The Official
Knit-a-Dress-a-Day
Knitting Book

The Official Knit-a-Dress-a-Day Knitting Book

by

JOAN RATTNER

Women's Editor, THIS WEEK MAGAZINE

GROSSET & DUNLAP
A NATIONAL GENERAL COMPANY
Publishers · New York

A Castle Books, Inc. Edition
Distributed To The Trade
By Book Sales, Inc.

Printed in the United States of America

Fifth Printing

In acknowledging the help she has received in the preparation of this book, the author expresses her thanks to Instruction Editor Molly Greenfeder, Advisor Dolly Martin, Illustrator Isabel Vaughan, and Miriam Morrison Peake.

Photographs by Stanley Conley.

Contents

Introduction

This is a book which had to be written because two million women asked for it. Just a few months ago I learned about a new and revolutionary way to knit FAST. A girl could start a dress in the morning and wear it at night. I wrote an article about it in **This Week Magazine** which appears in forty-three newspapers, offering free instructions for five dresses designed by Reynolds Yarns, Inc. To our amazement, over two million responses poured in, swamping us. Obviously, we hit upon something women were waiting for; there never was such a response to any offer in any publication. And everyone wanted MORE—hence this book with fifty sets of instructions for dresses and sweaters to knit in a hurry.

Here's the idea: Would you like to be the fastest knitter in town? You can knit a great dress in one day flat (or a sweater in less), using the new, revolutionary Instant Knitting method. It was invented for the girl in a hurry, the girl who always has seventeen things to do at once, who never had the time, the patience or the staying power to knit more than one sock or half a scarf. She may never have held a pair of knitting needles before. Now she can make herself an entire wardrobe in a week. With Instant Knitting, what used to take a week to make takes only a day. It's the Jet Age way of knitting, designed for the girl in a whirl.

Today, women like to make things but they like to make them quickly. They don't want to get involved in tedious, long-term projects—like knitting a dress the old-fashioned way in a few months. Most of us want things **now**—whether it's dinner, entertainment, coffee or clothes. Spend two weeks making a sweater? Never! We'd rather buy one. With life speeding by so fast and so much to do with it, we prefer to head downtown clutching our charge plates. But, wouldn't it be great, if we did have the time, to turn out a sweater made by our own hands?

With Instant Knitting, a girl (or her grandmother) can start a dress in the morning and wear it at night. She need only know the most elementary stitches which she will find right in this book.

Everybody's flipping over the knitting revolution. It's standing the yarn industry, long in the doldrums, on its ear. Invented by Reynolds Yarns, Inc., the secret to the new method is in the needles—great, huge, one-inch-round supersize needles. Called Jumbo Jets and made of hollow aluminum, these giant needles (as well as their cousins, the slightly smaller Junior Jumbo Jets) gobble up three to six strands of yarn at one time, making huge stitches (about one stitch per inch and one row per inch). The clothes they make, however, do not come out full of holes like Swiss cheese. The look can be quite bulky or remarkably fragile. You can make handsome men's sweaters as well as lacy shifts, bulky fishermen's knits or lightweight mohair dresses for little girls. In this book, we give you fifty sets of instructions from which to choose.

The big switch is the invention of Reynolds Yarns, Inc. and knitwear designer Jeanne Damon. A girl with a background of spectacular accomplishments, Miss Damon decided that the reason knitters were becoming fewer and farther between was that today's fast pace doesn't lend itself to time-consuming projects. The new generation wasn't knitting because it had too much else to do. "People want things yesterday, not next week. Knitting had to be made fast and fun," she said. She suddenly thought, "How about great big needles?" Off to her broom closet she went. Whittling away at a broomstick, she turned out a pair of inch-thick knitting needles. They worked! And they worked best with many strands of yarn at once, lapping them up at a rapid pace to produce great textures and color combinations. Each stitch was an inch big. Instead of six hundred stitches to cast on for a dress, about forty were needed. Whipping up a few samples on her broomsticks, she then took them to Tom Reynolds who knew a good thing when he saw it. A whole new concept was off the ground.

Reynolds, who is a long-time leader in the yarn industry, was delighted to find an idea sure to appeal to girls who had little time for holding knitting needles. He promptly had the broomsticks made in lightweight aluminum. Using Jeanne Damon's young designs, his company produced kits of yarns and instructions. The whole think took off like a rocket. Everyone was intrigued. Every newspaper and magazine in the country talked about the Reynolds' revolution. Yarn shops placed large orders. Lazy knitters perked up. Jeanne Damon appeared on TV and radio programs. **This Week Magazine** printed its story about Instant Knits, offering free instructions for five dresses, and received over two million requests. The stores promptly sold out. Reynolds stepped up deliveries and found a way to manufacture the needles faster. Now everybody's setting out to knit-a-dress-a-day.

The big news is that knitting has now jumped the generation gap. The kids, who left knitting to their grandmothers, are stripping yarn shop shelves bare. Even grandmothers are re-evaluating the time they spend tending to their knitting—thousands of them are already clicking with the giant needles and many strands of yarn.

In this book produced in cooperation with Reynolds Yarns, you'll find fifty dress and sweater designs. All are very easy to make and need absolutely no knitting experience. If you've never knit before, study the How-To-Knit section and you'll learn how in a hurry. If you have done some knitting, just be sure to read the Helpful Hints which will tip you off on working with the giant or junior giant needles. Always make a sample swatch first to get the feel of the needles and to check the size of your stitches.

Every design presented uses only basic stitches. Everything is aimed at giving you as few problems as possible. When you finish the garment, just sew the seams together. No pressing, no blocking. A date tonight and nothing to wear? Don't just sit there. Pick up your supersize needles and get to work. A few hours will solve your problem.

Join the knitting revolution. We promise you'll be an enthusiast tomorrow. And you'll have a new dress besides.

The Official
Knit-a-Dress-a-Day
Knitting Book

Abbreviations

Beg:	Beginning
Ch:	Chain
Dec:	Decrease
Inc:	Increase
K:	Knit
Lp:	Loop
P:	Purl
Pat:	Pattern
Rnd:	Round
Sc:	Single crochet stitch
Sl St:	Crocheted slip stitch
St:	Stitch
Sts:	Stitches
Stock:	Stockinette
Tog:	Together

How to Knit

CASTING ON.

METHOD 1. This is used to start a piece of knitting.

Step 1: Measure off about one yard from the end of yarn. * At this point make a slip-knot in the yarn and put it on the needle (Fig. 1). This is your first stitch.

Step 2: Using short end of yarn, make a loop over the left thumb (Fig. 2).

Step 3: Hold needle in right hand, insert tip of needle into front of thumb loop. Ball strand should be wrapped around little finger or threaded through fingers of right hand. With right forefinger, guide yarn around the tip of the needle from back to front (Fig. 3).

> * The length of yarn measured off before making slip-knot is determined by the size of needles, weight of yarn and number of stitches to be cast on. Allow the following length for each stitch you plan to cast on:

Size of Needles	Weight of Yarn	Length per Stitch
2-5	Light weight	½"
6-11	Versailles weight	1"
Jumbo Jets or Jumbo Juniors	Jumbo Jet combination	2"

1   2

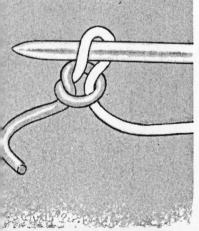
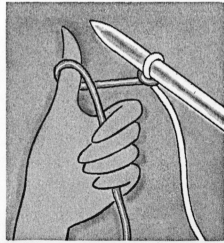

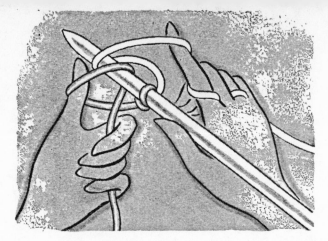

3

Step 4: Draw yarn through thumb loop (Fig. 4).

Step 5: Drop thumb loop and tighten short end (Fig. 5). Another stitch has been cast on. Repeat Steps 2, 3, 4, and 5 until desired number of stitches has been cast on.
If you use this method, start stockinette stitch with a purl row.

METHOD 2. This method may be used for starting a piece of knitting as well as adding stitches, replacing bound-off stitches over buttonholes, pockets, etc. To start a piece of knitting, make a slip-knot in the yarn, about 8″ from end, and put it on needle (Fig. 1). This counts as first stitch on left-hand needle.

Step 1: Hold needle with stitch in left-hand, other needle in right hand. Holding needle and yarn as described in Step 3 of Method 1, insert tip of right-hand needle from front to back through **first stitch on left-hand needle** (Fig. 6).

Step 2: With right forefinger, guide yarn from back to front under tip of right-hand needle (Fig. 7).

Step 3: Draw yarn through stitch on tip of left-hand needle (Fig. 8).

4   **5**

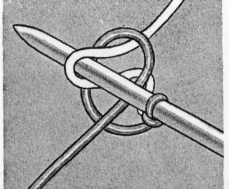

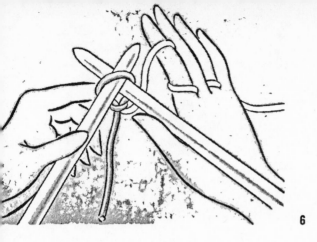

6

Step 4: Slip this stitch on tip of left-hand needle, withdraw right-hand needle, and tighten yarn (Fig. 9). A new stitch has been cast on left-hand needle. Repeat Steps 1, 2, 3, and 4 until the required number of stitches have been cast on.

If you use this method to start a piece of stockinette stitch, knit the first row through the back of loops.

KNITTING.

Step 1: Hold needle with the stitches in left-hand, free needle in right-hand. Hold needles and yarn as shown in Fig. 7, or in any position that feels comfortable and insures control of both needles and yarn. The closer right forefinger can be kept to the tip of the right-hand needle, less distance it will have to travel, and the more speed can be developed later. In Jumbo Jet knitting, you may find it easier to prop the left-hand needle against your lap.

Step 2: Insert tip of right-hand needle through front of first stitch on

7

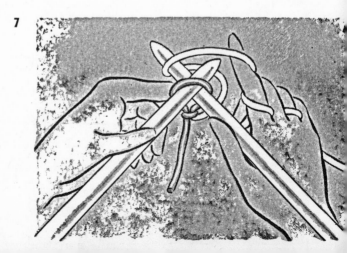

8

left-hand needle, guide yarn with the right forefinger from back to front under tip on right-hand needle (Fig. 10).

Step 3: Draw yarn through stitch on left-hand needle, making a stitch on right-hand needle (Fig. 11).

Step 4: Leave this stitch on right-hand needle and move the right-hand needle underneath the tip of left-hand needle and through original stitch on left-hand needle. Slip wool off left-hand needle. (Fig. 12). One stitch has been knitted from left-hand to right-hand needle. Keep stitches loose enough so that you can slide them along the needle, but firm enough so that they do not slide of their own accord. Repeat Steps 2, 3, and 4 until all stitches have been worked from left-hand to right-hand needle to complete one row. To start next row, turn right-hand needle around so that it becomes the left-hand needle.

10

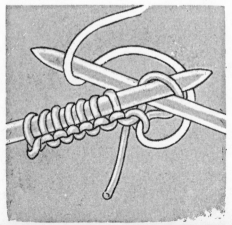

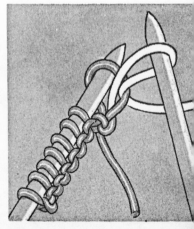

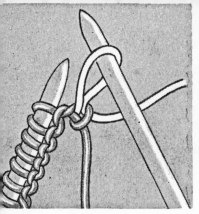

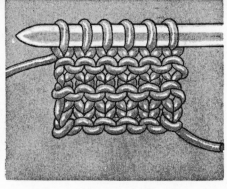

13

12

GARTER STITCH.

If you knit every row, the result will be the garter stitch (Fig. 13). It takes two rows to make one ridge on each side.

PURLING.

Step 1: With yarn in **front** of work, insert tip of right-hand needle **to you** through front of first stitch on left-hand needle (Fig. 14).

Step 2: Wrap yarn back over tip of needle and forward under needle (Fig. 15).

Step 3: Holding yarn tight, so it won't slip off, slide tip of right-hand needle back under left-hand needle, forming a new stitch on right-hand needle (Fig. 16).

Step 4: Leave this stitch on right-hand needle and drop the stitch through which it was drawn from left-hand needle. One stitch has been worked from left-hand needle to right-hand needle. Repeat Steps 1, 2, 3,

15

14

16

and 4 until all stitches have been worked to right-hand needle to complete one row. To start next row, turn right-hand needle around so that it becomes left-hand needle.

STOCKINETTE STITCH.

If you knit one row, then purl one row, alternately, the result will be the stockinette stitch. The knit side is the smooth side (Fig. 17), which is usually considered the right side of the work. If the purl, or nubby, side (Fig. 14) is used for the right side of the work, it is called a "reverse stockinette stitch." In Jumbo Jet knitting, if Method 1 of casting on has been used, stockinette stitch should start with a purl row. If Method 2 has been used for casting on, first row should be knitted by inserting needle into the back of each stitch (the part of loop behind left-hand needle).

RIBBING.

This is a combination of knit and purl stitches in one row. In the first row, follow the directions for alternating knit and purl stitches. After working the first row, the knit stitches (those with smooth side facing you) should be knitted; purl stitches (with nub side facing you) should be purled.

17

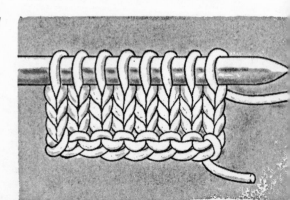

18

18

IMPORTANT: Yarn must be **in back** of right-hand needle before you knit a stitch or group of stitches, **in front** of right-hand needle before you purl a stitch or group of stitches. When you switch from knitting to purling, or vice versa, always pass yarn back and forth **under** tip of right-hand needle, otherwise you will get an extra stitch or an unsightly loose strand.

DECREASING.

METHOD 1: Knit (or purl) 2 stitches together as if they were one stitch (Fig. 18); one stitch has been decreased. This is written k 2 tog (or p 2 tog). If you knit (or purl) 3 stitches together, two stitches have been decreased. This is written k 3 tog (or p 3 tog). These decreases slant from left to right (Fig. 19).

METHOD 2: Insert right-hand needle through first stitch on left-hand needle as if to **knit**, but instead of knitting it, slip it off left-hand needle. Knit the next stitch. With tip of left-hand needle, lift the slipped stitch over the knit stitch and off the tip of needle (Fig. 20); one stitch has been decreased. This is written slip 1, k 1, psso (pass sl st over). To decrease 2 stitches, slip 1 stitch, knit 2 together, then lift slipped stitch over the last stitch on right-hand needle. This is written slip 1, k 2 tog, psso. These decreases slant from right to left (Fig. 21).

INCREASING.

METHOD 1: For increasing at an edge where increases will be hidden in

19

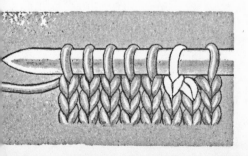

20

a seam, knit **and** purl in the same stitch before dropping it from left-hand needle.

METHOD 2: Knit in the back of the stitch and, before dropping it from left-hand needle, knit into the front of the same stitch.

METHOD 3: For making an increase in the body of work (such as darts on blouse or skirt, and raglan seams) knit (or purl) into the nub **below** next stitch, then knit next stitch. **On knit rows, the nub will be behind next stitch; on purl rows it will be in front of next stitch.** If working with several strands of yarn, knit into about half of the strands and then into remaining strands of the same stitch. This increase is practically invisible.

METHOD 4: For an increase that makes a decorative eyelet, wrap yarn once around needle between 2 stitches (Fig. 22). This is called yarn-over (yo). On the next row use this yarn-over (yo) as a stitch, forming an increase.

BINDING OFF.

This locks stitches securely in place and makes a finished edge.

Step 1: Knit (or purl) 2 stitches. With tip of left-hand needle, lift the first of these 2 stitches over last stitch (Fig. 23) and off the tip of the

21

right-hand needle (as shown in Fig. 24). One stitch has been bound off, one stitch remains on right-hand needle.

Step 2: Knit (or purl) another stitch so that there are again 2 stitches on right-hand needle; then lift first stitch over last stitch and off tip of needle. Another stitch has been bound off and one stitch remains on right-hand needle. Each stitch lifted off right-hand needle is a bound-off stitch. Repeat Step 2 until required number of stitches have been bound off. To bind off the last stitch on a row, cut yarn leaving an 8" end and draw cut end through remaining stitch. (Remember, it takes 2 stitches to bind off 1 stitch; for instance, if directions read: "k 6, bind off the next 4 sts, k 24...," knit 6 sts, then **knit 2 more** before starting to bind off. Bind off 4 times; the stitch remaining on right-hand needle now counts as the first stitch of next 24 stitches.

Helpful Hints for Instant Knits

General Information

HELPFUL HINTS TO REMEMBER WHEN MAKING INSTANT KNITS

1. Use yarns only in the combinations recommended. They have been especially selected for fit, color, design, and texture.

2. Keep all skeins separate as you work. Drop each ball into a box and pull out 3 or 4 yards at a time. Do not wind them all into a big ball; this will cause looping as you knit, and it is time-consuming when lengths have to be adjusted constantly.

3. It is important to make a sample swatch first, to get the "feel" of the new Jumbo Jet needles. Cast on at least 10 stitches and work in stockinette stitch for about 6". This is also essential for checking your gauge (to see if you are knitting too loosely or too tightly). Unless the gauge is right, the garment won't fit properly so make sure your stitches measure the same as given in the directions.

4. The first few rows on the skirt of a dress may look only wide enough for a sleeve, but after about 20 rows, knitting will ease out and be wide enough to fit perfectly (**if** your gauge is correct).

5. Follow instructions to the letter for good results.

6. Always knit, or purl the first and last stitch on every row, even when binding off; **never** slip the first stitch. Make all armhole or raglan decreases by knitting together the edge stitches. Pull the first and last stitches tight to make a firm edge, which will be easy to sew later.

7. Always join new yarn at the beginning of a row, never in the middle. Just start with a new strand, allowing a few inches to be woven in later. Any knot or spliced strand will show up later and make your work look amateurish.

8. When piece reaches underarms, always count the rows on the purl side and remember the number. Make sure that back and front and both sleeves have the same number of rows. Imagine what a big difference 2 or 4 rows would make, if each row measures 1"!

9. If you knit loosely, try to tighten up when working with Jumbo Jets. These needles are a new experience; it may take a few rows before you get the feel of them. Loose stitches will affect the appearance and size of your garment.

10. Roll up finished pieces instead of folding them.

NOW FOR THE FINISHING. This is important, so follow every step carefully.

1. Never block any Jumbo Jet garment; it isn't necessary.
2. Weave in all ends, one at a time, using a long yarn needle (not a crochet hook).
3. Rest garment on a table top, instead of your lap. Knitting may stretch, especially in humid weather, if it is allowed to drag before pieces are assembled.
4. For sewing (never crochet seams together), select yarn of the same color. If Monique yarn is used, split a strand in half. Avoid using nubby yarns, which are hard to work with.
5. Place pieces on table, wrong side up. Leave any part of the garment where purl nubs are on RIGHT side of work, to be sewed later. Starting at lower edge, sew side seams, catching together only the edge of each nub on matching rows. Use medium tension to allow plenty of give between stitches. Sew sleeve seams, then set in sleeves or sew raglan seams on wrong side in same way.
6. Turn garment right-side out. With one hand underneath, pinch seams together, and sew back and forth, taking one stitch on the right, one stitch on the left, alternately, at the sides of the groove over seam. Draw edges firmly together, closing up seam so that it practically disappears.
7. To seam the sections with purl nubs on right side, hold pieces right-side up. Start at lower edge, slip needle under a nub on one side, then under corresponding nub on other side. Pull the edges of the nubs together so that seams disappear.
8. Most edges are finished with a row of single crochet or crocheted slip-stitch. Work loosely and evenly on right side of garment; start at side or sleeve seam for body sections, at center back for collars.
9. "Ping-Pons" are ping-pong balls covered with crochet. Use a Size J hook and a single strand of yarn. Ch 3, join with sl st in first ch to form ring. **Rnd 1:** Ch 1, make 6 sc in ring. Join with sl st to first sc. **Rnd 2:** Make 2 sc in each sc around, join (12 sts). **Rnds 3 and 4:** Sc in each sc around, join. **Rnd 5:** Place ping-pong ball inside crocheted piece, * sc in next sc, pull up a loop in each of the next 2 sc, then draw yarn through all 3 loops on hook (1 sc decreased). Repeat from * around, join (6 sts). **Rnd 6:** Dec 1 sc around, fasten off. Sew up last rnd.
10. Jumbo Jet garments should be dry cleaned at a reliable dry cleaner's, not in a coin-operated machine. Instruct cleaner not to block or press.
11. Store your instant knits in a box or drawer instead of hanging in a closet.

Dresses for Women

Peek-a-Boo

Peek-a-Boo

■ **Sizes:** Directions are for small size (8-10). Changes for medium size (12-14) and large size (16-18) are in parentheses.
Fits Bust Size: 28-30 (32-34; 36-38)".

■ **Materials: Reynolds Monique** 7 (8-9) balls; Reynolds Scotch Mist 4 (4-5) balls.

■ **Knitting Needles Required:** 1 pair **Reynolds Jumbo Jets.** Aluminum crochet hook size J. Four ping-pong balls for ping-pon sleeve trim.

■ **IMPORTANT:** Before starting garment, see Helpful Hints and Sizing.

■ **Gauge:** 4 sts = 3¼"; 8 pat rows = 5". Make test piece in stockinette st for sizing (see Helpful Hints, No. 2). Rip and re-use piece.

■ **Back:** With 1 strand of each yarn held tog, cast on 21 (23-25) sts.
Row 1: K 1, * p 1, k 1. Repeat from * across. **Rows 2, 3 and 4:** Repeat row 1 for seed st stripe. **Rows 5-9:** K 1 row, p 1 row for stockinette st stripe. Repeat rows 2-9 for pat until total length is 24 (25-26)". Keep track of rows worked.
Raglan Armholes: Continue in pat, bind off 2 sts at beg of next 2 rows. Dec 1 st each end every other row until 7 sts remain. Bind off.

■ **Front:** Work same as back.

■ **Sleeves:** With 1 strand of each yarn, cast on 11 (13-13) sts. Work in pat as for back, inc 1 st each end every 2" 2 (2-3) times—15 (17-19) sts. Work even until sleeve measures 16½ (17-17½)".
Raglan Cap: Bind off 2 sts at beg of next 2 rows. Dec 1 st each end every 4th row once then every other row until 3 sts remain. Bind off.

■ **Finishing:** DO NOT STEAM OR BLOCK DRESS. With split length of Monique and right sides tog, weave sleeve caps to front and back armholes (see General Information). Weave side and sleeve seams. Right side facing, with 1 strand of each yarn, work 1 row slip st around neck just below bound-off neck sts. Join in first st and end off.

■ **Ping-pons** (make 4): With 1 strand of each yarn, wrap yarn over finger to form ring. **Rnd 1:** Insert hook in ring and pull up a loop, ch 1. Make 6 sc in ring. Mark ends of rnds. **Rnd 2:** 2 sc in back loop of each sc— 12 sc. **Rnd 3:** Sc in back loop of each sc. **Rnd 4:** Place over ping-pong ball, * pull up a loop in back loop of each of 2 sc, yarn over hook and draw through 3 loops on hook (dec). Repeat from * around—6 sc. Slip st in next sc. End off, leaving yarn to sew with. Sew up last rnd.
■ **Ties:** With 1 strand of each yarn, crochet two 36" chains. Run chains through wrist edges, 1 row above, with ends opposite seams. Trim ties with ping-pons.

Between Seasons

- **Sizes:** Directions are for small size (8-10). Changes for medium size (12-14) and large size (16-18) are in parentheses.
Fits Bust Size: 28-30 (32-34; 36-38)".

- **Materials: Reynolds Alpaca & Wool** 3 (3-4) balls; **Pontresina** 4 (5-6) balls; **French Floss** 2 (2-3) balls; **Mohair No. 1,** 3 (4-5) balls.

- **Knitting Needles Required: Reynolds Junior Jumbo Jets.**

- **IMPORTANT:** Before starting dress, see Helpful Hints and Sizing.

- **Gauge:** 3 sts = 2"; 2 rows = 1". Make test piece in stockinette st for sizing (see Helpful Hints, No. 2). Rip and re-use test piece.

- **Back:** With 1 strand of each yarn, cast on 27 (30-33) sts. Purl 1 row, k 1 row for 8 rows for reverse stockinette st border, k 1 row, p 1 row for 8 rows for stockinette st, then repeat first 8 rows once more. Work in stockinette st until total length is 23½ (24½-25½)". Keep track of rows worked.
Raglan Armholes: Bind off 2 sts at beg of next 2 rows. Dec 1 st each edge every 4th row once, then every other row until 17 (18-19) sts remain. Working in reverse stockinette st, continue to dec 1 st each edge every other row until 11 (12-13) sts remain. Bind off.

- **Front:** Work same as back to underarms.
Raglan Armholes: Bind off 2 sts at beg of next 2 rows. Dec 1 st each edge every 4th row once, every other row until 19 (20-21) sts remain. Working in reverse stockinette st, continue to dec 1 st each edge every other row until 13 (14-15) sts remain. Bind off.

- **Sleeves:** With 1 strand of each yarn, cast on 20 (22-24) sts. Work 8 rows reverse stockinette st, 4 (5-6) rows stockinette st.
Raglan Top: Bind off 2 sts at beg of next 2 rows. Dec 1 st each edge every 4th row twice, every other row 0 (1-2) times—12 sts on all sizes. Working in reverse stockinette st, dec 1 st each edge every other row 3 times. Bind off remaining 6 sts.

- **Finishing:** DO NOT STEAM OR BLOCK DRESS. With 1 strand Alpaca and Wool and right sides tog, weave sleeve caps to front and back armholes (see General Information). Weave side and sleeve seams.

28

Between Seasons

Miss Liberty

- **Sizes:** Directions are written for Small Size (8-10). Changes for Medium Size (12-14) and Large Size (16-18) are in parentheses.

- **Materials: Renynolds Pontresina** in three colors, 4 (5-5) balls MC, 1 (2-2) balls A, 1 ball B. **Royale Crylor** in three colors, 2 (3-3) balls MC, 1 ball A, 1 ball B. **Paloma** in three colors, 5 (6-6) balls MC, 1 (2-2) balls A, 1 ball B. **Mohair No. 1** in three colors, 4 (5-5) balls MC, 1 (2-2) balls A, 1 ball B.

- **Knitting Needles Required:** 1 pair **Reynolds Junior Jumbo Jets.** Aluminum crochet hook size K.

- **IMPORTANT:** Before starting garment, see Helpful Hints and Sizing.

- **Gauge:** 5 sts = 3"; 7 rows = 3".

- **Back:** With Reynolds Junior Jumbo Jet knitting needles and 4 strands of MC yarn (1 of each kind) cast on 28 (30-34) sts. Work even in stockinette st until 24½ (25½-26½) inches, or desired length to underarm.
Armhole: Bind off 2 (2-2) sts at beg of the next 2 rows. Dec 1 st each end every row until 12 (14-16) sts remain. Bind off, **AT SAME TIME** knitting 2 sts tog 6 (7-8) times.

- **Front:** Work same as Back to underarm.
Armholes: Bind off 2 (2-2) sts at beg of the next 2 rows. Dec 1 st each end every row until 12 (14-16) sts remain. Bind off, **AT SAME TIME** knitting 2 sts tog 8 (9-10) times.

- **Sleeves:** With Reynolds Junior Jumbo Jet knitting nedles and 4 strands of A yarn (1 of each kind) cast on 30 (32-34) sts. Starting with a knit row, work even in stockinette st for 6 rows. (This completes A stripe.) Break off A. Join 4 strands of MC yarn (1 of each kind). Knit one row. **Row 8:** Work in stockinette st, decreasing 1 st at each end of needle. Work even for 3 rows. This completes MC stripe. Break off MC yarn. Tie in 4 strands of B yarn (1 of each kind). Work in stockinette st for 4 rows. **Row 5:** Dec 1 st each end of needle. This completes B stripe. Break off B. Join 4 strands of MC yarn. Work in stockinette st for 5 rows. This completes MC stripe. Break off MC yarn. Join 4 strands of A yarn. Work in stockinette st for 2 rows. **Row 3:** Dec 1 st each end of needle. Work in stockinette st for 2 rows. This completes A stripe. Break off A yarn. Join 4 strands of MC yarn and work stockinette st for 5 rows. **Row 6:** Dec 1 st each end of needle. Continue in stockinette st (using MC yarn) until piece measures 17 (17½-18) inches in all, or desired length to underarm.

- **Armhole:** Bind off 2 (2-2) sts at beg of the next 2 rows. Dec 1 st each end every other row until 8 (10-12) sts remain. Bind off, AT SAME TIME knitting 2 sts tog 4 (5-6) times across row.

- **Scarf:** Using Junior Jumbo Jet knitting needles and 4 strands of A yarn cast on 108 sts. Work even in stockinette st for 5 rows. **Next row:**

Knit across for fold ridge. Break off A yarn. Join 4 strands of B yarn and work stockinette st for 5 rows. Bind off.

■ **Finishing:** With right sides together, wrong side facing you, using 1 strand of Royale Crylor (MC) weave side, sleeve and raglan seams. Turn dress right side out and using same yarn reweave seams, keeping work flat. Using No. K crochet hook and 4 strands of MC yarn work 1 row sc around bottom of dress and neck edge. Using same hook and 4 strands of A yarn work 1 row sc around bottom of sleeves. Fold scarf in half lengthwise. Using same hook and 3 strands of A yarn (1 Pontresina, 1 Royale Crylor and 1 Paloma) work 1 row sc completely around folded scarf.

Miss Liberty

Demure Miss

- **Sizes:** Directions are for small size (8-10). Changes for medium size (12-14) and large size (16-18) are in parentheses.
Fits Bust Size: 28-30 (32-34; 36-38)".

- **Materials: Reynolds Chanson de Paris** 3 (4-5) balls or **Alpaca & Wool** 2 (2-3) balls; **Super** Cabri 3 (4-5) balls; Monique 5 (6-7) balls in each of two other colors.

- **Knitting Needles Required: Reynolds Jumbo Jets.** Aluminum crochet hook size K, one ping-pong ball (for button) to close back neck.

- **IMPORTANT:** Before starting dress, see **Helpful Hints and Sizing.**

- **Back:** With 1 strand of each yarn (4) held tog, cast on 18 (20-22) sts.

- **Border:** Work in stockinette stitch (K 1 row, P 1 row) for 7 rows. Purl side is right side for border.) K 1 row, P 1 row. Hereafter, work in stockinette stitch (K 1 row, P 1 row) until piece measures 24½ (25-25½)" from beginning. (Keep track of rows worked.)
Raglan Armholes: Bind off 2 sts at beginning of next two rows. Work 2 rows even. Dec 1 st each end of needle next row. Purl back. Divide for neck opening 6 (7-8) sts each side. Continue to dec 1 st at armhole edge every other row until 3 (4-5) sts remain. Bind off. Work other side to correspond.

- **Front:** Work same as back for 24½ (25-25½) from beginning. Keep track of rows worked.

- **Raglan armholes:** Bind off 2 sts at beg of next 2 rows. Work two rows even. Dec 1 st each end of needle on next row, then every other row until 8 (10-12) sts remain. Bind off.

- **Sleeves:** With one strand of each yarn (4) held tog, cast on 13 (14-15) sts. Work in stockinette stitch (K 1 row, P 1 row) for 5 rows. Purl side is right side for border. K 1 row, P 1 row. **Raglan shaping:** Bind off 2 sts at beginning of next 2 rows. Work next 2 rows even. Dec 1 st each end of needle every other row until 3 (4-5) sts remain. Bind off. With 4 strands and K crochet hook, single crochet around neck edge.

- **Finishing:** DO NOT STEAM OR BLOCK. With split length of **Monique** and right sides tog, sew side seams and underarm seams, set sleeve in place easing raglan shaping. Right side facing, with the 4 strands, sc around neck edge.

- **Button:** With same 4 strands, wrap yarn over finger to form ring. **Rnd 1:** Insert hook in ring and pull up a loop, ch 1. Make 6 sc in ring. Mark ends of rnds. **Rnd 2:** Make 2 sc in back loop of each sc—12 sc. **Rnd 3:** Sc in back loop of each sc. **Rnd 4:** Place over ping-pong ball,* pull up a loop in back loop of each of 2 sc, yarn over hook and draw through 3 loops on hook (dec). Repeat from* around—6 sc. Slip st in next sc. End

Demure Miss

off, leaving yarn to sew with. Sew button to one corner of back neck. Make a crocheted chain for buttonloop; sew to corner opposite button.

■ **Collar:** With same 4 strands, cast on 28 sts. Work in stockinette st for 3 rows. Bind off. Weave short ends tog (with P side for right side). Fold collar in half, weave cast-on and bound-off edges tog. Can be worn as headband too.

Short Sleeve Waffle

- **Sizes:** Directions are for small size (8-10). Changes for medium size (12-14) and large size (16-18) are in parentheses.

- **Fits Bust Size:** 28-30 (32-34; 36-38)".

- **Materials:** **Reynolds** Alpaca & Wool 4 (5-6) balls; French Floss 2 (2-3) balls; Encore 6 (6-7) balls.

- **Knitting needles required:** 1 pair **Reynolds Junior Jumbo Jets.** Aluminium crochet hook size J. Two ping-pong balls for tie trim.

- **IMPORTANT:** Before starting dress, see Helpful Hints and Sizing.

- **Gauge:** 6 sts = 4½"; 5 rows = 2¼". Make test piece in stockinette st for sizing (see Helpful Hints, No. 2). Rip and re-use test piece.

- **Back:** With 2 strands Alpaca and 1 strand each of French Floss and Encore, cast on 21 (25-27) sts. **Pattern: Rows 1, 3, and 5:** K 3 (5-6), p 5, k 5, p 5, k 3 (5-6) sts. **Rows 2, 4, 6:** P 3 (5-6), k 5, p 5, k 5, p 3 (5-6) sts. **Row 7:** Repeat row 1 (one waffle row worked). **Mark first and last knit block on sides for right side of back piece.** Repeat rows 1-7 for pat (thus reversing every 7 rows) until there are 8 rows of waffles (56 rows). Total length should be about 25" to underarms.

- **Raglan Armholes:** Continue in pat, bind off 3 (3-4) sts at beg of next 2 rows. Dec 1 st each edge every other row 4 times—7 (11-11) sts. Bind off loosely, knitting the k sts and purling the p sts facing you.

- **Front:** Work as for back to underarms. **Note: On small size,** mark first and last knit block on pat row 7 for right side. **On medium and large sizes,** mark first and last purl block on pat row 6 for right side.

- **Raglan Armholes:** Continue in pat, bind off 3 (3-4) sts at beg of next 2 rows. Dec 1 st each side every other row 3 times. Bind off remaining 9 (13-13) sts.

- **Sleeves:** With same 4 strands, cast on 17 (19-21) sts. **Pattern: Rows 1, 3, 5:** P 1 (2-3), k 5, p 5, k 5, p 1 (2-3) sts. **Rows 2, 4 and 6:** K 1 (2-3), p 5, k 5, p 5, k 1 (2-3) sts. **Row 7:** Repeat row 1 (waffle row worked). Mark first and last ½ purl block at lower edge on sides for right side of sleeves. Repeat rows 1-4 once more.

- **Raglan Cap:** Continue in pat, bind off 3 (3-4) sts at beg of next 2 rows. Dec 1 st each edge every other row 3 (4-4) times—5 sts. Work 2 rows more on **Size 8-10 only. All Sizes:** Bind off in same manner as back neck.

- **Finishing:** DO NOT STEAM OR BLOCK. With 1 strand Alpaca and right sides tog, weave sleeve caps to front and back armholes (see General Information), matching rows; leave the 2 extra rows on front edge of

Short Sleeve Waffle

sleeve cap to form neck as pictured. Weave side and sleeve seams, matching pat. Right side facing, with same 4 strands, work 1 row sc around lower edge of dress; work 1 row around neck edge, so that back neck and bound-off edge of sleeve cap is high and front forms a triangle as pictured.

■ **Ties:** With same 4 strands, crochet two chains desired length; sew to V-points at front neck.

■ **Ping-pons** (make two): With same 4 strands, wrap yarn over finger to form ring. **Rnd 1:** Insert hook in ring and pull up a loop, ch 1. Make 6 sc in ring. Mark ends of rnds. **Rnd 2:** 2 sc in back loop of each sc—12 sc. **Rnd 3:** Sc in back loop of each sc. **Rnd 4:** Place over ping-pong ball, * pull up a loop in back loop of each of 2 sc, yarn over hook and draw through 3 loops on hook (dec.) Repeat from * around—6 sc. Slip st in next sc. End off, leaving yarn to sew with. Sew up last rnd. Sew ping-pons to ends of ties.

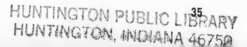
35

Short Sleeve Irish Fisherman

- **Sizes:** Directions are for small size (8-10). Changes for medium size (12-14) and large size (16-18) are in parentheses.

- Fits Bust Size: 28-30 (32-34; 36-38)".

- **Materials:** Reynolds Irish Fisherman Yarn, 16 (18-20) skeins.

- **Knitting Needles Required: Reynolds Junior Jumbo Jets.** Aluminum crochet hook size J. 1 ping-pong ball.

- **IMPORTANT:** Before starting dress, see Helpful Hints and Sizing.

- **Gauge:** 3 sts = 2"; 5 rows = 2". Make test piece in seed st for sizing (see Helpful Hints No. 2).

- **Cable Pattern:** Worked on 7 sts. **Row 1:** P 1, k 2, p 1, k 2, p 1. **Row 2:** K 1, p 2, k 1, p 2, k 1. **Row 3:** P 1, slip next st on crochet hook and hold in back of work, k next st, k 1 from hook **(cable twist made)**, p 1, make cable twist, p 1. **Row 4:** Repeat Row 2. Repeat these 4 rows for cable pat.

- **Tree of Life Pattern:** Worked on 9 sts. **Note:** Tbl = through back of loop. **Row 1:** P 3, k next 3 sts tbl, p 3. **Row 2:** K 3, p 3 tbl, k 3. **Row 3: P 2,** slip next st on hook and hold in back of work, k 1 tbl, p 1 from hook **(k is moved to right)**, k 1 tbl, slip next st on hook and hold in front of work, p next st, k 1 tbl from hook **(k st moved to left)**, p 2. **Row 4:** K 2, p 1 tbl, k 1, p 1 tbl, k 1, p 1 tbl, k 2. **Row 5:** P 1, move k st to right, p 1, k1 tbl, p 1, move k st to left, p 1. **Row 6:** K 1, p 1 tbl, k 2, p 1 tbl, k 2, p 1 tbl, k 1. **Row 7:** Move k st to right, p 2, k 1 tbl, p 2, move k st to left. **Row 8:** P 1 tbl, k 3, p 1 tbl, k 3, p 1 tbl. Repeat Rows 3 through 8 for pattern.

- **Back: Rows 1-10:** With 3 strands yarn held tog, cast on 27 (31-35) sts. **Row 1:** K 1, * p 1, k 1. Repeat from * across. Repeat Row 1 for seed st, taking care always to k the sts with p side facing you and p the sts with k side facing you, until 6 rows have been worked. (K 1 row, p 1 row) twice. **Row 11:** K 3, * in next st make k 1, p 1, k 1, p 1 and k 1 for popcorn, turn, p 5, turn, k 5, turn, p 5, turn, pass the 2nd 3rd 4th and 5th sts over the first st on left-hand needle, k this first st and next 4 (5-6) sts. Repeat from * ending with k 3 after last popcorn; there are 5 popcorns with 4 (5-6) sts between them and 3 sts at each edge. **Rows 12-15:** (p 1 row, k 1 row) twice. **Rows 16-20:** Work 5 rows st, ending on wrong side. **Aran Pattern: Row 1:** Work 2 (4-6) sts in seed st, slip a loop of colored yarn on needle for a marker, work 7 sts cable, slip another marker on needle, work 9 sts tree pat, marker, 7 sts cable, marker, 2 (4-6) sts seed st. **Note:** Slip markers on every row. **Row 2:** Work 2 (4-6) sts seed st, 7 sts cable, 9 sts tree pat, 7 sts cable, 2 (4-6) sts seed st. Keeping pats as established, work even until total length is 24 (24½-25)" or desired length to underarms. Keep track of rows worked.

- **Raglan Armholes:** Keeping pat sequence, bind off 1 (2-3) sts at beg of next 2 rows. Work 2 rows. Dec 1 st each edge every other row until 11 (11-13) sts remain. Bind off.

- **Front:** Work same as back until raglan armholes have been decreased to 13 (13-15) sts. Bind off.

- **Sleeves:** With 3 strands of yarn cast on 19 (21-23) sts. **Rows 1-10:** Work 6 rows seed st. (K 1 row, p 1 row) twice. **Row 11:** K 3 (4-5), * popcorn in

Short Sleeve Irish Fisherman

next st, k 5. Repeat from * until 3 popcorns have been made, k 3 (4-5).
Rows 12-16: (P 1 row, k 1 row) twice. Work 1 row seed st, ending on wrong side.

■ **Raglan Top:** Working in seed st, bind off 1 (2-3) sts at beg of next 2 rows. Work 2 rows. Slip markers on needle on each side of the center 9 sts. Working tree pat between markers and other sts in seed st, dec 1 st each and every other row until 5 sts remain. Bind off.

■ **Collar:** With 3 strands yarn cast on 27 sts. P 1 row, k 1 row, p 1 row. **Row 4** (right side): K 6, * popcorn, k 6. Repeat from * until 3 popcorns have been made, k 6. P 1 row, k 2 rows. Bind off, purling the sts.

■ **Garters:** With 3 strands yarn cast on 21 sts. P 1 row, k 1 row, p 1 row. **Row 4** (right side): K 3, * popcorn, k 6. Repeat from * until 3 popcorns have been made, k 3. P 1 row, k 2 rows. Bind off, purling the sts.

■ **Finishing:** DO NOT STEAM OR BLOCK DRESS. With 1 strand of yarn weave in sleeves and ease in raglan shaping; weave side and sleeve seams (see General Information). Weave ends of graters tog. With 3 strands yarn work 1 row sc evenly around all edges of dress. From k side, work 1 row sc and 1 row sl st, below sc row, around cast-on edges of garters. From k side, work sc along one short end of collar, across cast-on edge and other short end, ch 1, turn. Sc in first sc, ch 10 for buttonloop, sc in opposite corner, ch 1 turn. Make 10 sc over buttonloop, sl st in next sc. Fasten off. Work 1 row sl st on long edge, below sc row. Using 2 strands yarn, make ping-pon (see General Information) and sew to end of collar opposite buttonloop.

Joan of Arc

Joan of Arc

- **Sizes:** Directions are for small size (8-10). Changes for medium size (12-14) and large size (16-18) are in parentheses.
- **Fits Bust Size:** 28-30 (32-34); 36-38)". **Hips:** 30-32 (34-36; 38-40)".
- **Materials: Reynolds Feu D'Artifice,** 8 (9-10) balls each of two colors or 16 (18-20) balls of one color.
- **Knitting needles: Reynolds Junior Jumbo Jets.** Aluminum crochet hook size K. Two ping-pong balls.
- **IMPORTANT:** Before starting dress, see **Helpful Hints and Sizing.**
- **NOTE:** Purl side is right side of dress and hat.
- **Dress: Back:** With 3 strands of each color (6) held tog, cast on 26 (28-30) sts. Work in stockinette st (K 1 row, P 1 row) for 23½ (24½-25½)" or desired length to underarm. Keep track of rows worked.
- **Raglan Armholes:** Bind off 3 sts at beg of next 2 rows. Dec 1 st each edge every other row until 10 (10-12) sts remain. Purl back next row. Bind off loosely.
- **Front:** Work same as back until raglan armholes have been reduced to 12 (12-14) sts. Purl back next row. Bind off loosely.
- **Sleeves:** With same 6 strands, cast on 31 (33-35) sts. Work in stockinette st (K 1 row, P 1 row) dec 1 st each edge on every 6th row, 3 times, every 4th row 2 times—21 (23-25) sts. Work until total length is 16½ (17-17½)" or desired length to underarms.
- **Raglan Cap:** Bind off 3 sts at beg of next 2 rows. Dec 1 st each edge every other row until 5 (5-7) sts remain. Bind off loosely.
- **Finishing:** DO NOT STEAM OR BLOCK DRESS. With 1 strand of yarn, weave body seams and sleeve seams (See General Information). With 6 strands and K crochet hook, set sleeves in, easing raglan shaping to fit.
- **Hat:** With 3 strands of each color, cast on 22 sts. Work in Stockinette for 3 rows.
- **Next row:** Continue working in stockinette. Dec 1 st each end of needle every 3rd row 3 times. Then continue in stockinette, dec 1 st end of needle every other row 3 times.
- **Next row:** (P—row). Dec 1 st each end of needle every row 3 times. (You now have 2 sts left). Bind off remaining two sts.

Single crochet around triangle using 6 strands and K crochet hook, chain two 23" ties for hat. Crochet covers for two ping-pong balls. Sew to one end of each tie and sew other end of each tie to front corners of triangle.
Note: Remember P side is right side of triangle.

Reverie

- **Sizes:** Directions are for small size (8-10). Changes for medium size (12-14) and large size (16-18) are in parentheses.

- **Fits Bust Size:** 28-30 (32-34; 36-38)".

- **Materials: Reynolds Versailles** 5 (6-7) balls; **Highland Fling** 3 (4-5) balls; **Mohair No. 1,** 4 (5-6) balls; **Super Cabri** 4 (5-6) balls.

- **Knitting Needles Required:** 1 pair **Reynolds Jumbo Jets.** Aluminum crochet hook size J. Large-eyed sewing needle.

- **IMPORTANT:** Before starting garment, see Helpful Hints and Sizing.

- **Guage:** 6 sts = 5"; 2 rows = 1". Make test piece in stockinette st for sizing (see Helpful Hints, No. 2). Rip and re-use test piece.

- **Dress:** Starting at lower front edge with 6 strands held together (2 Versailles, 2 Mohair No. 1, 1 Highland Fling and 1 Super Cabri), cast on 20 (22-24) sts. **Row 1** (right side as worn by 2 models; 3rd switched the back to the front): K 10 (11-12) sts, p 10 (11-12) sts. Repeat this row for lower section of pat and work for 12½ (13-13½)". Mark last row on work. **Next Row:** P 10 (11-12), k 10 (11-12) sts. Repeat this row for reversed pat until total length is 24 (25-26)". Keep track of rows worked.

- **Sleeves:** Keeping to pat as established, cast on 4 (5-6) sts at beg of next 2 rows, 6 sts at beg of next 4 rows — 52 (56-60) sts. Work 3 (4-5) rows in p 26 (28-30), k 26 (28-30) pat.
- **Neck:** P 23 (25-27) sts, bind off loosely in pat (p 3, k 3) center 6 sts, finish row. Work last set of sts, finish row. Work last set of sts for 5 rows, ending at neck edge, break yarn, leave sts on needle. Starting at neck edge work other set of 23 (25-27) sts for 5 rows.

- **Back: Next Row:** Work to neck edge, cast on 6 sts for back neck, work across sts of other side — 52 (56-60) sts. Work 4 (5-6) rows in p 26 (28-30), k 26 (28-30) pat.

- **Sleeves:** Bind off 6 sts at beg of next 4 rows, 4 (5-6) sts at beg of next 2 rows — 20 (22-24) sts. Work even for same number of rows as on front from underarm to marked row. Work lower section of pat in k 10 (11-12), p 10 (11-12) pat for same number of rows as on front to lower edge. Bind off in pat same tension as sts.

- **Finishing:** DO NOT STEAM OR BLOCK DRESS. With 1 strand of Versailles and right sides tog, weave side and sleeve seams (see General Directions). Right side facing, with the 6 strands, work 1 row sc around neck and sleeve edges; 1 row slip st around lower edge of dress.

Reverie

Chamois

- **Sizes:** Directions are for small size (8-10). Changes for medium size (12-14) and large size (16-18) are in parentheses.
- **Fits Bust Size:** 28-30 (32-34; 36-38)".
- **Materials: Reynolds Scotch Mist** 6 (7-8) balls light color for stripes; Monique 6 (6-7) balls in each of two other colors.
- **Knitting Needles Required: Reynolds Jumbo Jets.** Aluminum crochet hook size J.
- **IMPORTANT:** Before starting dress, see Helpful Hints and Sizing.
- **Gauge:** 6 sts = 5"; 5 rows = 3". Make test piece in stockinette st for sizing (see Helpful Hints, No. 2). Rip and reuse test piece.
- **Wind 2 balls of Scotch Mist into 6 balls.**
- **Back:** With 1 strand of each color, cast on 19 (22-25) sts. **Row 1** (wrong side): Knit. **Row 2:** Prul. * Drop yarns, attach 6 strands of Scotch Mist. P 2 rows, k 1 row, p 1 row (3 ridges on right side of work). Break off Scotch Mist, pick up original 3 strands. Purl 3 rows (1 ridge on right side) * . K 1 row, p 1 row twice, purl 1 row on right side. Repeat from * to * once more. Now work in stockinette st, until total length is 25 (25½-26)". Keep track of rows worked.
- **Raglan Armholes:** Bind off 2 sts at beg of next 2 rows. Dec 1 st each side every 3rd row once, then every other row until 7 (8-9) sts remain. Bind off.
- **Front:** Work same as back until 9 (10-11) sts remain on raglan armholes. Bind off.
- **Sleeves:** With 3 strands of yarn (1 of each color) cast on 13 (14-15) sts. Work same as back until both Scotch Mist stripes have been completed. With original 3 strands, purl 3 rows. Work in stockinette st, increasing 1 st at each edge every 4th row once — 15 (16-17) sts. Work even until total length is 17 (17-17½)".
- **Raglan Top:** Bind of 2 sts at beg of next 2 rows. Work even for 0 (2-4) rows, dec 1 st each edge on the next row and again every 3rd row twice, every other row until 3 (4-5) sts remain. Bind off.

- **Finishing:** NO NOT STEAM OR BLOCK DRESS. With split strand of one Monique and right sides tog, weave sleeve caps to front and back armholes (see General Information). Weave side and sleeve seams. Fasten off ends of yarn on wrong side by overcasting them securely with sewing thread. Turn cast-on edges to wrong side, leaving 1 ridge below first stripe, and sew. With 3 colors, work 1 row sc and 1 row loose sl st around neck.

Highland Lassie

- **Sizes:** Directions are for small size (8-10). Changes for medium size (12-14) and large size (16-18) are in parentheses.
- **Fits Bust Size:** 28-30 (32-34; 36-38)".
- **Materials: Reyonlds Super Cabri** 3 (4-4) balls; **Monique** 6 (7-8) balls light color and **Monique** 9 (10-11) balls dark color.
- **Knitting Needles Required: Reynolds Jumbo Jets.** Aluminum crochet hook size J. Four ping-pong balls for trim.
- **IMPORTANT:** Before starting dress, see Helpful Hints and Sizing.
- **Gauge:** 6 sts = 5"; 5 rows = 3". Make test piece in stockinette st for sizing (see Helpful Hints, No. 2). Rip and re-use test piece.
- **Back:** With 1 strand Super Cabri and 1 strand each of light and dark Monique, cast on 18 (20-22) sts. Work even in stockinette st for 24½ (25-25½)". Keep track of rows worked.
- **Raglan Armholes:** Bind off 2 sts at beg of next 2 rows. Dec 1 st each edge every 3rd row 3 (2-1) times, then every other row 0 (2-4) times, Bind off loosely remaining 8 sts.
- **Front:** Work same as back.
- **Sleeves:** With same 3 strands of yarn, cast on 15 (16-17) sts. Work even in stockinette st for 16½ (17-17½)".
- **Raglan Top:** Bind off 2 sts at beg of next 2 rows. Dec 1 st each edge every 3rd row 1 (2-3) times, then every other row 3 (2-1) times. Bind off loosely remaining 3 (4-5) sts.
- **Hem:** With 2 strands darker color Monique, cast on 44 (48-52) sts. Work in stockinette st for 5 rows. Bind off loosely.
- **Collar:** With 2 strands darker Monique, cast on 30 (32-34) sts. Work in stockinette st for 4 rows. Bind off.
- **Cuffs:** With 2 strands darker Monique, cast on 21 (22-23) sts. Work same as collar.
- **Garters:** With 2 strands darker Monique, cast on 13 (14-15) sts. Work same as collar.
- **Finishing:** DO NOT STEAM OR BLOCK DRESS. With split length of one Monique and right sides together, weave sleeve caps to front and back armholes (see General Information). Weave side and sleeve seams.
Join ends of hem, collar, cuffs and garters. Sew knit side of one edge of hem just under edge of dress, then roll up hem to right side and tack other edge in place. Sew on collar and cuffs the same way. Roll

Highland Lassie

up garters, purl side out, and sew long edges together, inserting eleastic if desired.

■ **Ping-pons** (make 2): With 1 strand of light Monique, wrap yarn over finger to form ring. **Rnd 1:** Insert hook in ring and pull up a loop, ch 1. Make 6 sc in ring. Mark ends of rnds. **Rnd 2:** Make 2 sc in back loop of each sc — 12 sc. **Rnd 3:** Sc in back loop of each sc. **Rnd 4:** Place over ping-pong ball, * pull up a loop in back loop of each of 2 sc, yarn over hook and draw through 3 loops on hook (dec). Repeat from * around — 6 sc. Slip st in next sc. End off, leaving yarn to sew with. Sew up last rnd.

■ **Ties:** With 2 strands of darker Monique, make crochted chain 24″ long, tie in a bow, attach bow to garter and sew ping-pons to ends of chain.

Estrellita

- **Sizes:** Directions are for small size (8-10). Changes for medium size (12-14) and large size (16-18) are in parentheses.
- **Fits Bust Size:** 28-30 (32-34; 36-38)".
- **Materials: Reynolds Danskyarn** 4 (5-6) balls; **Kirsti** 3 (4-4) balls; Estrellita 6 (7-7) balls.
- **Knitting needles required: Reynolds Jumbo Jets.** Aluminum crochet hook size J. 4 ping-pong balls.
- **IMPORTANT:** Before starting dress, see Helpful Hints and Sizing.
- **Gauge:** 4 sts = 3"; 5 rows = 3". Make test piece in stockinette st (see Helpful Hints, No. 2). Rip and re-use test piece.
- **Back:** With 1 strand of each yarn (3), held tog, cast on 21 (24-27) sts loosely. Work in stockinette st (k 1 row, p 1 row) for 24 (24½-25)", or desired length to underarms. Keep track of rows worked.
- **Raglan Armholes:** Bind off 3 sts at beg of next 2 rows. Work 2 rows. Dec 1 st each edge every other row until 9 (10-11) sts remain. Bind off loosely.
- **Front:** Work same as back until armholes have been decreased to 11 (12-13) sts.
- **Neck:** Work 2 sts, drop yarn; join 1 strand of each yarn and bind off center 7 (8-9) sts, finish row. On the 2 sts of each side work 1 more row, K 2 tog, fasten off.
- **Sleeves:** With same 3 strands yarn cast on 17 (18-19) sts. Work in stockinette st for 14 (14½-14½)". **Note:** Cuff adds 4" to sleeve length.
- **Raglan Top:** Bind off 3 sts at beg of next 2 rows. Dec 1 st each edge every other row until 3 (2-2) sts remain. Bind off loosely.
- **Collar:** Starting at outer edge with same 3 strands yarn, cast on loosely 61 (65-69) sts. K 2 rows, p 1 row, k 1 row. **Row 5** (right side): K 1, * yo, k 2 tog. Repeat from * across. **Row 6:** Repeat row 5. P 1 row, k 1 row. Bind off, working sts as follows: K 1, * k 2 tog. Repeat from * across.
- **Cuffs:** Starting at outer edge with same 3 strands yarn cast on 33 (37-41) sts. Work same as collar.
- **Finishing:** DO NOT STEAM OR BLOCK DRESS. Weave raglan armhole seams (see General Information), side and sleeve seams. Sew on collar and cuffs with purl side for right side. With same 3 strands yarn, make two crocheted chains about 35" long. Run these chains through sleeves just above cuffs. Make two ping-pons (see General Information) and sew to ends of chain.

Estrellita

College Cable

- **Sizes:** Directions are for small size (8-10). Changes for medium size (12-14) and large size (16-18) are in parentheses.
- **Fits Bust Size:** 28-30 (32-34; 36-38)".
- **Materials:** Reynolds Pontresina 5 (5-6) balls; **French Floss** 3 (3-4) balls; **Super Cabri** 6 (7-7) balls.
- **Knitting needles required: Reynolds Junior Jumbo Jets.** Aluminum crochet hook size J. Two ping-pong balls.
- IMPORTANT: Before starting dress, see Helpful Hints and Sizing.
- **Gauge:** 7 sts = 4¼"; 7 rows = 3½". Make test piece in stockinette st for sizing (see Helpful Hints No. 2). Rip and e-use test piece.
- **Back:** With 1 strand of each yarn (3 strands), cast on 26 (30-32) sts. Work in stockinette st for 24 (24½-25)", or desired length to underarms. Keep track of rows worked.
- **Raglan Armholes:** Bind off 3 sts at beg of next 2 rows. Dec 1 st each edge every other row until 8 (10-10) sts remain. Bind off.
- **Front:** With 1 strand of each yarn cast on 28 (30-34) sts. **Row 1:** K 8 (9-11), p 1, k 1, p 1, k 6 for cable, p 1, k 1, p 1, k 8 (9-11). **Row 2:** P 8 (9-11), k 1, p 1, k 1, p 6, k 1, p 1, k 1, p 8 (9-11). **Rows 3 and 4:** Repeat Rows 1 and 2. **Row 5:** K 8 (9-11), p 1, k 1, p 1, slip next 3 sts on crochet hook and hold in back of work, k next 3 sts, k 3 from crochet hook **(cable twisted on 6 sts)**, p 1, k 1, p 1, k 8, (9-11). **Rows 6, 7 and 8:** Repeat Rows 2, 1 and 2. Repeat these 8 rows for cable pat until piece measures same as back to underarms.
- **Raglan Armholes:** Bind off 3 sts at beg of next 2 rows. Dec 1 st each edge every other row until 12 (12-14) sts remain. Bind off.
- **Sleeves:** With 1 strand of each yarn cast on 20 (22-22) sts. **Row 1:** K 4 (5-5), p 1, k 1, p 1, k 6 for cable, p 1, k 1, p 1, k 4 (5-5). **Row 2:** P 4 (5-5), k 1, p 1, k 1, p 6, k 1, p 1, k 1, p 4 (5-5). **Rows 3 and 4:** Repeat Rows 1 and 2. Twisting cable over the center sts as for back on the next row and again every 8th row, work even in pat for 6". Inc 1 st each edge on the next row and again every 4½" 1 (1-2) times more—24 (26-28) sts. Work even until total length is 17 (17½-17½)".
- **Raglan Top:** Bind off 3 sts at beg of next 2 rows. Dec 1 st each edge every other row until 6 sts remain. Bind off 3 sts at beg of right side rows twice for right sleeve; 3 sts at beg of wrong side rows for left sleeve.
- **Collar:** With 1 strand each yarn cast on 10 sts. **Row 1** (right side): K 2, p 1, k 4, p 1, k 2. **Row 2:** P 2, k 1, p 4, k 1, p 2. **Rows 3 and 4:** Repeat Rows 1 and 2. **Row 5:** K 2, p 1, slip next 2 sts on crochet hook and hold in back, k next 2 sts, k 2 from crochet hook **(cable** twisted on 4 sts), p 1, k 2. **Row 6:** Repeat Row 2. Repeat these 6 rows until piece measures 21 (22-23)". Bind off.

■ **Finishing:** DO NOT STEAM OR BLOCK DRESS. With 1 strand Pontresina weave raglan, side and sleeve seams (see General Information). With all 3 strands work 1 row sc evenly around neck, sleeves and lower edge, and 1 row around collar making 3 sc in each corner. **Ping-pons:** Cover ping-pong balls with crochet (see General Information). Sew to corners at one end of collar; make crocheted chains for buttonloops on opposite end.

College Cable

Discotheque

Discotheque

- **Sizes:** Directions are for small size (8-10). Changes for medium size (12-14) and large size (16-18) are in parentheses.
- **Fits Bust Size:** 28-30 (32-34; 36-38)".
- **Materials:** Reynolds Monique 5 (6-6) balls in each of two colors; in matching or coordinating colors **Reynolds Chanson de Paris** 3 (4-4) balls **or Versailles** 3 (4-4) balls and **Super Cabri** 3 (4-4) balls.
- **Knitting Needles Required: Reynolds Jumbo Jets.** Aluminum crochet hook size J.
- **IMPORTANT:** Before starting dress, see Helpful Hints and Sizing.
- **Gauge:** 6 sts = 5"; 4 rows (2 ridges) = 2". Make a test piece in garter st (k each row) on 6 sts for 8 rows. Piece should measure 5" × 4". Rip and re-use test piece.
- **Back:** With 1 strand of each yarn (4) cast on loosely 18 (20-22) sts. Work even in garter st (k every row; 2 rows = 1 ridge) until piece measures 25 (25½-26)". Mark last row. Keep track of rows worked.
- **Armholes:** Bind off 2 sts at beginning of next 2 rows. Work 1 row. **Next Row:** Dec 1 st each end of needle—12 (14-16) sts.
- **Back Opening:** Work first 6 (7-8) sts. Turn and work these sts until armhole measures 5½ (6-6½)" above marked row. End at center back.
- **Neck:** Bind off 3 (3-4) sts at center back edge. Finish row. Turn and bind off remaining 3 (4-4) sts. Attach yarn at center back and work other side to correspond.
- **Front:** Work same as back to underarm. Mark last row.
- **Armholes:** Bind off 2 sts at beginning of next 2 rows. Work 1 row even. **Next Row:** Dec 1 st each end of needle—12 (14-16) sts. Work even until 5½ (6-6½)" above armhole.
- **Neck:** Work first 3 (4-4) sts; bind off loosely; center 6 (6-8) sts, finish row. Turn; bind off 3 (4-4) sts. Attach yarn at neck edge and bind off 3 (4-4) sts.

- **Finishing:** DO NOT STEAM OR BLOCK DRESS. With split strand of one Monique, weave side and shoulder seams (see General Information). Right side facing, with the same 4 strands, work 1 row sc loosely around neck and armholes and 1 row around lower edge of dress if desired.
- **Ping-Pon:** With the same 4 strands, cover one ping-pong ball with crochet (see General Information). Sew ping-pon to one corner of back neck. Make crocheted chain for buttonloop on other corner to close.

51

All-in-One Dress

- **Sizes:** Directions are for small size (8-10). Changes for medium size (12-14) and large size (16-18) are in parentheses.
- **Fits Bust Size:** 28-30 (32-34; 36-38)".
- **Materials: Reynolds Place Concorde** 5 (6-7) balls; **Royale Crylor** 2 (3-3) balls; **Alpaca & Wool** 2 (3-3) balls.
- **Knitting needles required: Reynolds Jumbo Jets.** Reynolds Jumbo Jet Crochet Hook. 2 ping-pong balls.
- IMPORTANT: Before starting dress, see Helpful Hints and Sizing.
- **Gauge:** 6 sts = 5"; 5 rows = 3". Make test piece in stockinette st for sizing (see Helpful Hints No. 2). Rip and re-use test piece.
- **Dress:** Starting at lower edge of back with 1 strand of each yarn (3 strands), cast on 20 (22-24) sts. Work in stockinette st for 20½ (21-21½)". Keep track of rows worked. **Note:** Crocheted border worked later—adds 4" to length. Mark last row.
- **Armholes:** Bind off 2 (2-3) sts at beg of next 2 rows. Work even on 16 (18-18) sts for 6 (6½-6½)" above marked row.
- **Neck:** Work 5 (6-6) sts, bind off center 6 sts, finish row. Work 3 more rows on the last 5 (6-6) sts, ending at neck edge. Break off yarn. Starting at opposite neck edge, work other side for 4 rows, ending at neck edge, cast on 6 sts for front of neck, work across other side. Work even on 16 (18-18) sts until piece measures 12 (12½-13)" above marked row. Cast on 2 (2-3) sts at beg of next 2 rows for underarms. Work even on 20 (22-24) sts until piece measures 20½ (21-21½)" from underarms. Bind off.
- **Sleeves:** With k side facing you and same 3 strands of yarn, pick up and k 19 (20-22) sts evenly around armhole edge. Starting with a purl row, work in stockinette st for 12 (12½-13)". Bind off. Crocheted Border adds 3" to length.
- **Finishing:** DO NOT STEAM OR BLOCK DRESS. With one strand of Royale Crylor or Alpaca, weave side and sleeve seams (see General Information).
- **Hem:** With 2 strands of Place Concorde and Jumbo Jet Hook, ch 43 (45-47) to fit around lower edge of dress. Join with sl st in first ch, forming a ring. **Rnd 1:** Ch 1, sc in same place as sl st and each ch. Join with sl st in back loop of first sc; be careful not to work into sl st or ch-1 of joining. **Rnd 2:** Ch 1, sc in same place as sl st and back loop of each sc, join. **Rnds 3 and 4:** Repeat Rnd 2. Fasten off. Sew to lower edge of dress.

■ **Cuffs:** Starting with ch 19 (20-21), work same as hem for 3 rnds. Fasten off. Sew in place.

■ **Collar:** Starting with ch 22, work same as hem for 3 rnds. Fasten off. Sew to neck.

■ **Belt:** With 2 strands of Place Concorde make a chocheted chain 82" long or desired length. Fasten off. With 1 strand Place Concorde cover 2 ping-pong balls with chochet (see General Information), sew to ends of belt.

All-in-One Dress

Sugar and Spice

- **Sizes:** Directions are for small size (8-10). Changes for medium size (12-14) and large size (16-18) are in parentheses.
- **Fits Bust Size:** 28-30 (32-34; 36-38)".
- **Materials: Reynolds Pontresina** 4 (5-5) balls; **Paloma** 6 (6-7) balls; **Super Cabri** 5 (6-6) balls.
- **Knitting needles required: Reynolds Jumbo Jets.** Aluminum crochet hook size J. Large hook end eye.
- **IMPORTANT:** Before starting dress, see Helpful Hints and Sizing.
- **Gauge:** 4 sts = 3"; 5 rows = 3". Make test piece in stockinette st (see Helpful Hints, No. 2). Rip and re-use test piece.
- **Back:** With 1 strand of each yarn (3 strands) held tog, cast on 21 (24-27) sts. Work in stockinette st (k 1 row, p 1 row) for 24½ (25-25½)", end with p row. Keep track of rows worked.
- **Raglan Armholes:** Bind off 2 sts at beg of next 2 rows. Work 2 rows. Dec 1 st at each edge of next row, then every other row until 11 (12-13) sts remain. Bind off.
- **Front:** Work same as back until raglan armholes have been decreased to 13 (14-15) sts.
- **Neck:** Work 2 sts, drop yarn; join 1 strand of each yarn (3) and bind off center 9 (10-11) sts, finish row. On each of the remaining 2 sts work 1 more row, work 2 tog, fasten off.
- **Sleeves:** With same 3 strands yarn, cast on 15 (16-18) sts. Work in stockinette st for 8 rows.
- **Raglan Top:** Work as for back raglan armholes until 5 (4-4) sts remain. Bind off.
- **Collar:** With 3 strands yarn cast on 34 (38-42) sts. Work in stockinette st for 6 rows. Bind off. **Purl side is right side.**
- **Cuffs:** With 3 strands yarn cast on 16 (17-18) sts. Work same as collar.
- **Belt:** With 3 strands yarn cast on 41 (45-49) sts. Work same as collar. Belt can be used for hem if longer length is desired.
- **Bow:** Work same as collar.
- **Finishing:** DO NOT STEAM OR BLOCK DRESS. Weave raglan seams, side ,and sleeve seams (see General Information). With same 3 strands yarn, sc around lower edge of dress. With purl side as right side, join ends of collar and cuffs, long edges of belt and bow. Fold collar in half and weave edges to neck and sleeves, forming rolls. Fold bow to form 2 loops and 2 ends. Sew to one end of belt. Close belt with hook and eye.

Sugar and Spice

Triple Monique

■ **Sizes:** Directions are for small size (8-10). Changes for medium size (12-14) and large size (16-18) are in parentheses.

■ **Materials:** Reynolds Monique 6 (7-7) balls each of three different colors.

■ **Knitting Needles Required:** 1 pair **Reynolds Jumbo Jets**. Aluminum crochet hook size J. Two ping-pong balls for ping-pon cap trim.

■ **IMPORTANT:** Before starting garment, see Helpful Hints and Sizing.

■ **Gauge:** 6 sts = 5½"; 3 rows = 2". Make test piece in stockinette st for sizing (see Helpful Hints, No. 2). Rip and re-use test piece.

■ **DRESS: Back:** With 1 strand of each color held together, cast on 18 (20-22) sts. Work in stockinette st for 23 (24-25)". Keep track of rows worked.
■ **Raglan Armholes:** Bind off 2 sts at beg of next 2 rows. Dec 1 st each end every 4th row once, then every other row until 6 (8-8) sts remain. Bind off.

■ **Front:** Work same as back until reglan armholes have been decreased to 8 (10-10) sts. Bind off.

■ **Sleeves:** With 1 strand of each color, cast on 10 (10-12) sts. Work in stockinette st, inc 1 st each and every 2" 2 (3-3) times—14 (16-18) sts. Work even until sleeve measures 16½ (17-17½)".
■ **Raglan Cap:** Work as back raglan armholes until 4 sts remain. Bind off.

■ **Finishing:** DO NOT STEAM OR BLOCK DRESS. With split length of Monique and right sides tog, weave sleeve caps to front and back armholes (see General Information). Weave side and sleeve seams. Right side facing, with the 3 colors, work 1 row slip st around neck, 1 row sc around lower edge and sleeves.

■ **TRIANGLE CAP:** With 1 strand of each color, cast on 18 sts. Work in stockinette st for 4 rows. Dec 1 st each end on next row, then every 3rd row twice. Continue to dec 1 st each end **every** row until 2 sts remain. Work 2 sts tog, fasten off. Right side facing, with the 3 colors, work 1 row slip st around edge of triangle with 3 sc in each corner. Join with slip st in first sc, end off.

■ **Ping-pons** (make 2): With 1 strand of each color, wrap yarn over finger to form ring. **Rnd 1:** Insert hook in ring and pull up a loop, ch 1. Make 6 sc in ring. Mark ends of rnds. **Rnd 2:** Make 2 sc in back loop of each sc—12 sc. **Rnd 3:** Sc in back loop of each sc. **Rnd 4:** Place over ping-pong ball, * pull up a loop in back of each 2 sc, yarn over hook and draw through 3 loops on hook (dec). Repeat from * around—6 sc. Slip st in next sc. End off, leaving yarn to sew with. Sew up last rnd.

■ **Ties:** With the 3 colors, crochet two 27″ chains. Sew ties to sides at front of cap. Trim ties with the ping-pons.

Triple Monique

Ribbon Striped Dress

■ **Sizes:** Directions are written small size (8-10), changes for medium size (12-14) and large size (16-18) are parentheses.

■ **Materials:** 1 Pair Reynolds Jr. Jumbo Jet knitting needles

#J aluminum crochet hook		#5036 Pontresina	(2)
#2324 Dansk	(6)	#4638 Monte Carlo	(2)
Purple Jeweltone ribbon	(2)	Red Jewelton ribbon	(2)
#5021 Pontresina	(3)	#5025 Pontresina	(1)
#4601 Monte Carlo	(2)	#4611 Monte Carlo	(2)
White Jeweltone ribbon	(3)	Blue Jeweltone Ribbon	(1)

■ **Gauge:** 3 sts. = 2 inches; 5 rows = 2 inches

Using **Reynolds Jr. Jumbo Jet** knitting needles and 3 strands of yarn
■ **Back: (Dansk)** and 1 strand of ribbon, 4 strands of purple in all, cast on 28 (30-32) sts. Work in stock. st. for 28 (30-32) rows. Break off purple. Tie in white 3 strands of yarn (2 **Monte Carlo** and 1 **Pontresina**) and 1 strand of white ribbon. Work stock. st. 9 rows. Break white. Tie in red, 3 strands yarn (2 **Monte Carlo, 1 Pontresina**) and 1 strand ribbon. Stock. st. 10 rows. Break red. Tie in white same combination as before. Stock. st. 9 rows. Break white; tie in blue. 3 strands yarn (2 Monte Carlo, 1 Pontresina) and 1 strand ribbon. Work stock. st. for 4 (4-4) rows. Work will measure about 24 (25-26) inches.
■ **Armhole:** Bind off 3 (3-3) sts. at beg. of the next 2 rows. Work 2 rows even. Dec. 1 st. each end every other row until 12 (14-14) sts. remain. At same time that there are 10 rows blue, break off blue and tie in white same combination as before and finish piece in white. Bind off.

■ **Front:** Work same as back.

■ **Sleeve:** Using Reynolds Jr. Jumbo Jet knitting needles and 3 strands of purple yarn and 1 strand of purple ribbon, cast on 22 (24-26) sts. Work striping pattern as on body of dress. 9 (11-13) rows purple, 9 rows white, 10 rows red, 9 rows white and 4 rows blue. Sleeve will measure about 16¼ (17¼-18¼) inches.
■ **Armhole:** Bind off 3 (3-3) sts. at beg. of the next 2 rows. Work 2 rows even. Dec. 1 st. each end every other row until 6 (8-8) sts. remain. At same time that there are 10 rows blue, break off blue, tie in white same combination as before, finish sleeve in white. Bind off.

■ **Collar:** Using Jr. Jumbo Jet knitting needles and 3 strands of red yarn (same combination as before) and 1 strand of red ribbon, cast on 26 sts., all sizes. Work in stock. st. for 8 rows all sizes. Bind off.

■ **Hood:** Using Jr. Jumbo Jet knitting needles and purple combination, cast on 26 sts. all sizes. Work in stock. st., as follows, 8 rows purple, 4 rows white, 6 rows red, break off red. Join white combination and work 4 rows, decreasing 1 st. each end every other row. Join blue, dec. 1 st. each end of next row. Work 1 row even. K2 tog., across row. Work 1 row even. K2 tog. across row. Next row P1, P3 tog., P1. Bind off.

■ **Cap Peak:** Using Jr. Jumbo Jet knitting needles and purple combination, cast on 12 sts. Work in stock. st. Work 2 rows. Bind off 2 sts. at beg. of each of the next 4 rows. Bind off last 4 sts.

■ **Finishing:** With right sides together, wrong side facing you, using 1 strand of Monte Carlo or Dansk to match stripe, weave side sleeve and raglan seams, matching pattern rows. Turn dress right side out and re-weave seams. Using #J crochet hook and 1 strand of ribbon and 1 strand of Dansk or Pontresina in correct color, work 1 row sc around bottom of dress, sleeves, and neckline. Using 1 strand of ribbon and 1 strand of red yarn work 1 row sc around collar making a chain for button loop on one end. Using 3 strands red yarn, 1 strand of red ribbon, cover a ping pong ball (see ping pon note) and sew to the other end of collar for button.

■ **Finishing Cap:** Join shaped edge of cap peak to dec. edge of hood. Using 1 strand yarn, 1 strand ribbon in correct colors, work 1 row sl. st. over joining. Using 1 strand yarn and 1 strand ribbon in matching colors, work 1 row sc around hood.

■ **Hood Ties:** Using 4 strands of Monte Carlo, 2 strands ribbon in Blue, #J crochet hook, make 2 chains each 21 inches long. Attach 1 end to hood at front corners for ties.

Ribbon Striped Dress

Gold Metallic and Paillettes

Gold Metallic and Paillettes

Sizes: Directions are written for small size (8-10), changes for medium size (12-14) and large size (16-18) are in parentheses.

- **Material:** 1 Pair Reynolds Jr. **Jumbo Jet** knitting needles, 1 #J aluminum crochet hook, #Gold—**Gold Jeweltone** Ribbon (5), Color OR Lurex (9), 513 **Pailletees**—Round gold

- **Gauge:** 2 rows = 1 inch; 3 sts = 2 inches

- **Back:** String about 130 paillettes onto 3 strands of lurex and 1 strand of ribbon used together as 1 strand. Using Jr. Jumbo Jet knitting needles and the prepared yarn and ribbon, cast on 24 (26-28) sts. Knit 1 row. Next row * K1, bring a paillette up and hold against back of work as you knit the next st. Repeat across row from *. Knit 1 row. Next row * K1, with paillette, K1, repeat across row from *, repeat these 4 rows until there are 9 rows of paillettes. Take off any paillettes left over. Work even in stock. st. until piece measures 26 (27-28) inches.

- **Armhole:** Bind off 2 (2-2) sts. at beg. of the next 2 rows. Work 2 rows even. Dec. 1 st. each end every other row until 12 (14-14) sts. remain. Bind off as follows, K1, K2 tog. as you bind off, K the last st. to bind off.

- **Front:** Work same as back to underarm.

- **Armhole:** Bind off 2 (2-2) sts. at beg. of the next 2 rows. Work 2 rows even. Dec. 1 st. each end until 14 (16-16) sts. remain. Bind off same as back.

- **Sleeves:** Work same as back until border is completed. Dec. 1 st. each end of next row all sizes. Continue in stock st., dec. 1 st. each end every 6th row twice more all sizes 18 (20-22) sts., work even until 15 (16-17) inches.

- **Armhole:** Bind off 2 (2-2) sts. at beg. of the next 2 rows. Work 2 rows even. Dec. 1 st. each end every other row until 6 (8-8) sts. remain. Bind off as follows, K first st, K2 tog. across row as you bind off, K last st and bind off.

- **Collar:** String paillettes as before onto 3 strands of lurex and 1 strand of ribbon. Using Jr. Jumbo Jet knitting needles and the prepared yarn, cast on 28 (30-32) sts. Work same as border on dress and sleeves until there are 2 rows with paillettes. Bind off using paillettes.

- **Finishing:** Using #J crochet hook and 3 strands of lurex and 1 strand of ribbon (4 strands in all), work 1 row sc around bottom of dress and sleeves. Work 1 row sc around neckline, holding in to 18 (18½-19) inches. Using same hook and yarns, work 1 row sc around collar. Make a chain on one end for button loop. Using the same combination of yarn and ribbon, cover a ping pong ball. See ping pon note. Attach ping pon to other end of collar.

Beat-the-Band Dress

■ **Sizes:** Directions are written in small size (8-10), changes for medium size (12-14) and large size (16-18) are in parentheses.

■ **Materials:** 1 Pair **Junior Jumbo Jet** knitting needles; 1 #J aluminum crochet hook; #4613 **Monte Carlo** (2); #5033 **Pontresina** (2); **Emerald Jeweltone** Ribbon (2); #4633 **Monte Carlo** (2); #5035 **Pontresina** (2); **Jet Black Jeweltone** Ribbon (2); #4601 **Monte Carlo** (4); #5021 **Pontresina** (4); White patent **Jeweltone** Ribbon (4)

■ **Gauge:** 3 sts. = 2 inches; 5 rows = 2 inches

■ **Back:** Using Jr. Jumbo Jet knitting needles and 3 strands of yarn (2 strands of Monte Carlo and 1 of Pontresina in black) and 1 strand of black ribbon, 4 strands in all, cast on 28 (30-32) sts. Work in stock. st. for 10 rows. Break off black. Join 3 strands of white yarn (2 strands of Monte Carlo and 1 of Pontresina) and 1 strand of white ribbon. Work 6 rows of white. Break off white. Join 3 strands of green yarn (2 of Monte Carlo and 1 of Pontresina) and 1 strand of green ribbon. Work 8 rows of green. Break off green. Tie in 3 strands of white yarn and 1 strand of white ribbon same combination as before, continue in stock. st. until 24½ (25½-26½) inches, or desired length to underarm.

■ **Armhole:** Bind off 3 (3-3) sts. beg. of the next 2 rows. Work 2 rows even. Dec 1 st. each end every other row until 12 (14-14) sts. remain. Bind off.

■ **Front:** Work same as Back.

■ **Sleeves:** Using Jr. Jumbo Jet knitting needles and 3 strands of black yarn (2 of Monte Carlo and 1 of Pontresina) and 1 strand of black ribbon, 4 strands in all, cast on 26 (28-30) sts. Work in stock. st. for 10 rows. Break off black. Join same combination in white and work 6 rows. Break off white. Join green in same combination. Work 4 rows green. Next row dec. 1 st. each end all sizes. Work 3 more rows green. (8 rows green in all.) Break off green. Join white in same combination and work 6 rows in white. Next row dec. 1 st. each end all sizes. Work even on 22 (24-26) sts. until sleeve measures 16½ (17½-18½) inches or desired length to underarm.

■ **Armhole:** Bind off 3 (3-3) sts. at beg. of the next 2 rows. Work 2 rows even. Dec. 1 st. each end every other row until 6 (8-8) sts. remain. Bind off.

■ **Scarf:** Using Jr. Jumbo Jet knitting needles and black combination (4 strands), cast on 100 sts. all sizes. Work in stock. sts. for 5 rows. Knit next P row to make turning ridge. Break off black yarn. Join green combination (4 strands), knit first row, work in stockinette st. for 5 rows. Bind off.

■ **Finishing:** With right sides together, wrong side facing you, using 1 strand of Monte Carlo in the color to be joined, weave side, sleeve and

Beat-the-Band Dress

raglan seams. Turn dress right side out and keeping colors to match, reweave seams. Keep work flat. Using #J crochet hook and 1 strand of Monte Carlo in black and 1 strand of black ribbon (2 strands) work 1 row sc around bottom of dress and sleeves. Using same hook and 1 strand white ribbon, work 1 row sc around neck line.

Fold scarf in half lengthwise, on turning ridge. Using J crochet hook and 1 strand of Monte Carlo black and 1 strand black ribbon, work 1 row sc completely around scarf. Using same hook and yarn and ribbon work 1 row sl. st. into the row of knitting just below the sc row.

The following are the second and third color choices for this dress. The amounts are for the largest sizes.

COMBINATION #2—Purple, red and white

#2324 Dansk (3 strands)	6
Royal Purple Jeweltone Ribbon	2
#4638 Monte Carlo (2 strands)	2
#5036 Pontresina (1 strand)	2
#4601 Monte Carlo (2 strands)	5
White Patent Jeweltone Ribbon	4
#5021 Pontresina (1 strand)	4
Scarlet Jeweltone Ribbon	2

COMBINATION #3—Blue, green and white

#5021 Pontresina (1 strand)	4
#4601 Monte Carlo (2 strands)	5
White Patent Jeweltone Ribbon	4
#5033 Pontresina (1 strand)	2
#4613 Monte Carlo (2 strands)	2
Emerald Jeweltone Ribbon	2
#5025 Pontresina (1 strand)	2
#4611 Mone Carlo (2 strands)	2
Sapphire Jeweltone Ribbon	2

Women's Puff Sleeve Dress

Women's Puff Sleeve Dress

■ **Sizes:** Directions are for small size (8-10). Changes for medium size (12-14) and large size (16-18) are in parentheses.
Fits Bust Size: 28-30 (32-34; 36-38)".

■ **Materials: Reynolds Paloma** 4 (5-5) balls; **Reynolds Alpaca** and Wool 2 (3-3) balls; Reynolds Versailles 2 (3-3) balls.

■ **Knitting Needles Required: Reynolds Junior Jumbo Jets.** Aluminum crochet hook size J.

■ **IMPORTANT:** Before starting dress, see Helpful Hints and Sizing.

■ **Gauge:** 5 sts = 3"; 5 rows = 2". Make test piece in stockinette st (see Helpful Hints No. 2).

■ **Back:** With 1 strand of each yarn (3 strands), cast on 34 (37-40) sts. Work in stockinette st, decreasing 1 st each edge every 4" 5 times—24 (27-30) sts. Work even until total length is 23 (23½-24)". Keep track of rows worked.
Raglan Armholes: Bind off 3 sts at beg of next 2 rows. Work 2 rows even. Dec 1 st each end of next row, then every other row until 12 (13-14) sts remain. Bind off.

■ **Front:** Work same as back.

■ **Sleeves:** With same 3 strands cast on 17 (18-19) sts. K 1 row. **Row 2:** K in back and in front of each st across—34 (36-38) sts. **Row 3:** * K 1, k in front and back of next st. Repeat from * across—51 (54-57) sts. **Row 4, 5 and 6:** Knit each row.
Cap Shaping: Rows 1 and 2: Knitting every row, bind off 3 sts at beg of next 2 rows. **Row 3:** K 0 (1-1), * k 2 tog, k 1, k 2 tog. Repeat from * 8 (8-9) times, end with k 0 (2-0)—27 (30-31) sts. **Row 4:** K 1 (0-1), then k 2 tog across—14 (15-16) sts. **Row 5:** Dec 1 st each end of row. Bind off remaining 12 (13-14) sts.

■ **Finishing:** DO NOT STEAM OR BLOCK DRESS. Using 1 strand of Versailles, weave sleeves to armholes (see General Information), then weave side and sleeve seams. Right side facing, with 3 strands work 1 row sc evenly around lower edge and neck, keeping A-line at bottom of dress and square shape of neck.

Metallic A-Line

■ **Sizes:** Directions are written for small size (8-10). Changes for medium size (12-14) and large size (16-18) are in parentheses.

■ **Package Contains: Feu D'Artifice** (3 strands) #OR (9); **Jeweltone** Ribbon #Gold-Gold (5).

■ **Knitting Needles Required:** 1 pair **Reynolds Junior Jumbo Jet** Knitting needles; 1 #I aluminum crochet hook; 1 #K aluminum crochet hook; 4 ping-pong balls.
IMPORTANT: Before starting dress, see Helpful Hints and Sizing.

■ **Gauge:** 5 sts = 3", 7 rows = 3"

■ **Back:** Using Reynolds Junior Jumbo Jet knitting needles and 3 strands of Feu D'Artifice and 1 strand of Jeweltone Ribbon, cast on 33 (35-37) sts. Work even in stockinette st for 9 (9-9) rows. On next row, dec 1 st each end. Continue in stockinette st, decreasing 1 (1-1) st each end of every 9th (10th-10th) row, until there are 23 (25-27) sts on needle. Work even in stockinette st until piece measures 23½ (24½-25½) inches, or desired length to underarm.
Armhole: Bind off 3 (3-3) sts at the beginning of the next 2 rows. Work even in stockinette st for 2 (2-2) rows. Dec 1 st each end every other row until 9 (9-11) sts remain. Bind off.

■ **Front:** Work same as Back to underarm.
Armhole: Bind off 3 (3-3) sts at the beginning of the next 2 rows. Work even in stockinette st for 2 (2-2) rows. Dec 1 st each end every other row until 11 (11-13) sts remain. Bind off.

■ **Sleeve:** With Reynolds Junior Jumbo Jet knitting needles and 3 strands of Feu D'Artifice and 1 strand of Jeweltone Ribbon, cast on 27 (29-31) sts. Work even in stockinette st for 8 (8-8) rows. On next row dec 1 st each end. Continue in stockinette st, decreasing 1 st each end every 8 (9-9) rows until there are 21 (23-25) sts. Work even until sleeve measures 16½ (17½-18½) inches, or desired length to underarm.
Armhole: Bind off 3 (3-3) sts at the beg of the next 2 rows. Work even for 2 (2-2) rows. Dec 1 st each end every other row until 7 (7-9) sts remain. Bind off.

■ **Finishing:** Place pieces of garment so right sides are together, and wrong side faces you. Using one strand of Feu D'Artifice, weave side, sleeve and raglan seams. Turn dress right side out. Using one strand of Feu D'Artifice reweave seams on right side. Using #I crochet hook and 3 strands of yarn and 1 strand of ribbon, work 1 row sc around bottom of dress and sleeves. Work 1 row sc around neck edge. Sc over 4 ping pong balls using a #K crochet hook and 3 strands of yarn and 1 strand of ribbon. (see note on Ping Pon in General Information.) Using same hook and yarns, make 2 chains each 34" in length. Attach the Ping Pons to the ends of chains. Tie chains around upper arm.

Metallic A-Line

Long Sleeve Irish Fisherman

- **Sizes:** Directions are for small size (8-10). Changes for medium size (12-14) and large size (16-18) are in parentheses.
Fist Bust Size: 28-30 (32-34; 36-38)".

- **Materials:** Reynolds Irish Fisherman Yarn 21 (23-24) skeins.
Knitting needles required: Reynolds Junior Jumbo Jets. Aluminum crochet hook size J.
IMPORTANT: Before starting dress, see Helpful Hints and Sizing.

- **Gauge:** 3 sts = 2"; 5 rows = 2". Make test piece in double seed st for sizing (see Helpful Hints No. 2).

- **Twisted Ribbing: Row 1:** P 1, *k 1 in back of stitch, p 1, repeat from * across. **Row 2:** K 1, * p 1 in back of stitch, k 1, repeat from * across. Repeat these 2 rows.

- **Berry Stitch** (worked on 9 sts): **Row 1:** Purl. **Row 2:** K 1; (k 1, p 1, k 1 in the same stitch for berry), p 3 tog, make berry, p 3 tog, k 1. **Row 3:** Purl. **Row 4:** K 1. p 3 tog, berry, p 3 tog, berry, k 1. Repeat these 4 rows.

- **Double Seed: Row 1:** K 1, p 1. **Row 2:** P 1, k 1. **Row 3:** P 1, k 1. **Row 4:** K 1, p 1. Repeat these 4 rows.

- **Cable** (worked on 9 sts): **Row 1:** K 9. **Row 2:** P 9. **Row 3:** Sl 3 sts to dp needle and hold in back of work, k 1, k 3 sts from dp needle, k1, sl 1 and hold in front of work, k 3, k 1 from dp needle. **Row 4:** P 9. Repeat these 4 rows.

- **Back:** With 3 strands held tog, cast on 29 (33-37) sts. Work 8 rows in twisted ribbing.
Aran Pattern: Work 2 sts double seed, 6 (8-10) sts berry stitch, 2 sts twisted ribbing, 9 sts in cable, 2 sts twisted ribbing, 6 (8-10) sts berry stitch, 2 sts double seed. Work in Aran pat as established until work measures 24¾" or desired length to underarm.
Raglan Armholes: Keeping in pat, bind off 2 (2-3) sts at beg of next 2 rows. Work 2 rows even. Dec 1 st each end of needle every other row until 11 (13-15) sts remain. Bind off loosely.

- **Front:** Work as for back until raglan armholes have been decreased to 13 (15-17) sts. Bind off loosely.

- **Sleeves:** With 3 strands of yarn, cast on 17 sts. Work 8 rows in twisted ribbing, inc 1 st each end of last row—19 sts.
Aran Pattern: Work 2 sts double seed st, 2 sts twisted ribbing, 9 sts in cable, 2 sts twisted ribbing, 2 sts double seed st. Work in Aran pat as established, inc 1 st each end every 8th row 1 (2-3) times, working added sts in double seed st pat—21 (23-25) sts. Work even until sleeve measures 17" from start or desired length to underarm.
Raglan Top: Bind off 2 (2-3) sts at beg of next 2 rows. Work 2 rows even. Dec 1 st each end every other row until 5 (5-5) sts remain. Bind off loosely.

■ **Finishing:** DO NOT STEAM OR BLOCK DRESS. With 1 strand of yarn weave in sleeves and ease in raglan shaping; weave side and sleeve seams (see General Information).

■ **Collar:** Cast on 49 sts. Work in twisted ribbing for 12". Bind off in ribbing. Weave side edges tog, forming a ring. Fold collar in half and weave cast-on and bound-off edges tog, allowing enough ease to go over head. Sew collar to neck.

Long Sleeve Irish Fisherman

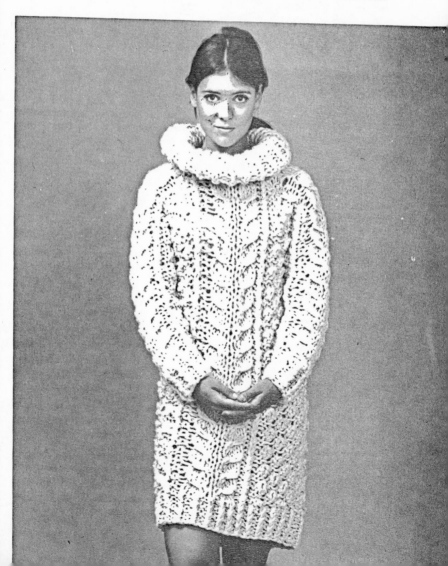

Poodle Dress

■ **Sizes:** Directions are written for a small size (8-10). Changes for medium size (12-14) and large size (16-18) are in parentheses.

■ **Materials:** 1 pair **Reynolds Jr. Jumbo Jet** knitting needles; 1 #K aluminum crochet hook; Dress #1 - #1720 **Monique** (15); Dress #2 - #1718 **Monique** (15)

■ **Gauge:** 8 sts. − 5 inches, 2 rows = 1 inch

■ **Back:** Using Reynolds Jr. Jumbo Jet knitting needles and 2 strands of yarn· (both strands same color) cast on 26 (28-30) sts. Work in stockinette st (starting with a knit row) for 8 rows. **Next row:** Purl (this will reverse the stock st). Continue in stock st for 4 rows more. **Next row:** Purl (this will reverse the stockinette again). Work in stock st for 5 rows more. Reverse stockinette once again (knit side will be right side), and work until piece measures 24½ (25½-26½) inches, or desired length to underarm.

■ **Armhole:** Bind off 3 (3-3) sts at the beg of the next 2 rows. Work 2 rows even. Dec. 1 st each end of needle every other row until 14 (16-18) sts remain. Continuing to decrease 1 st each end every other row, purl next knit row (this will reverse stockinette). Work until 8 (10-10) sts are on needle and there are 6 (6-8) purl "bumps" on right side. Bind off.

■ **Front:** Work same as back to underarm.

■ **Armhole:** Bind off 3 (3-3) sts at the beg of the next 2 rows. Work 2 rows even. Dec. 1 st each end of needle every other row until 16 (18-20) sts remain, continuing to decrease 1 st each end every other row; purl next knit row. This will reverse stockinette. Work in stock. st until 10 (12-12) sts remain and there are 6 (6-8) purl "bumps" on right side of work. Bind off.

■ **Sleeve:** With Reynolds Jr. Jumbo Jet knitting needles and 2 strands of yarn, cast on 18 (20-22) sts. Work in stock st for 8 rows, (starting with a knit row). **Next row:** Purl (this will reverse stock st) Work in stock st for 4 rows more. **Next row:** Purl (this will reverse stock st again) Work in stock st for 5 rows more. Reverse stock once more (knit side is new right side) and work until piece measures 16½ (17½-18½) inches or desired length to underarm.

■ **Armhole:** Bind off 3 (3-3) sts at beg of next 2 rows. Work 2 rows even. Dec. 1 st each end of needle every other row until 10 (10-12) sts remain. Continuing to decrease 1 st each end every other row, purl next knit row to reverse stockinette. Work in stock st until 4 (4-4) sts remain and there are 6 (6-8) purl "bumps" on right side of work. Bind off.

■ **Finishing:** With right sides together, wrong side facing you, using split strand of Monigue, weave side, sleeve and raglan seams, matching pat-

Poodle Dress

tern rows. Turn work right side out and reweave seams. Using #K crochet hook and 2 strands of yarn, work 1 row sc around bottom of dress and sleeves. Also around neck edge.

■ **Garters:** Using Reynolds Jr. Jumbo Jet knitting needles and 2 strands of yarn, cast on 22 sts all sizes). Work in stockinette st for 4 rows. Bind off.

■ **Finishing:** Using one split strand of Monique, sew short ends of garters together. Purl side is right side.

71

Sweaters for Women

Ribbed Sweater

- **Sizes:** Directions are written for small size (8-10). Changes for medium size (12-14) and large size (16-18) are in parentheses.

- **Materials: For Sweater: Reynolds Pontresina** 3 (4-5) balls; **French Floss** 1 (2-3) balls; **Plumage** 4 (5-6) balls. **For Collar: Reynolds Pontresina 2** balls; **French Floss** 1 ball; **Plumage** 2 balls.

- **Knitting Needles Required:** 1 pair **Reynolds Junior Jumbo Jets.** Aluminum crochet hook size J.

- **IMPORTANT:** Before starting garment, see Helpful Hints and Sizing.

- **Gauge:** 5 sts = 3½"; 5 rows = 2".

- **Back:** Using Reynolds Junior Jumbo Jet knitting needles and 3 strands of yarn (1 of each kind) cast on 23 (25-27) sts. **Row 1** (right side): P 4 (5-6), K 5, P 5, K 5, P 4 (5-6). **Row 2:** K 4 (5-6), P 5, K 5, P 5, K 4 (5-6). Repeat these 2 rows alternatively until piece measures 17 (18-19) inches, or desired length to underarm.
Armhole: Keep pattern as established. Bind off 2 sts at beg of the next 2 rows. Work 2 rows even. Dec 1 st each end every other row until 7 (9-9) sts remain. Bind off.

- **Front:** Using Reynolds Junior Jumbo Jet knitting needles and 3 stands of yarn (1 of each kind) cast on 23 (25-27) sts. **Row 1** (right side): K 4 (5-6), P 5, K 5, P 5, K 4 (5-6) sts. **Row 2:** P 4 (5-6), K 5, P 5, K 5, P 4 (5-6). Repeat these 2 rows alternately until piece measures 17 (18-19) inches or desired length to underarm.
Armhole: Keep pattern as established. Bind off 2 sts at beg of the next 2 rows. Work 2 rows even. Dec 1 st each end every other row until 9 (11-11) sts remain. Bind off.

- **Sleeve:** Using Reynolds Junior Jumbo Jet knitting needles and 3 strands of yarn (1 of each kind) cast on 13 (15-15) sts. **Row 1** (right side): P 4 (5-5), K 5, P 4 (5-5) sts. **Row 2:** K 4 (5-5), P 5, K 4 (5-5) sts. Repeat these 2 rows alternately for 5 (5-4) inches. End with right side row. **Next row,** inc 1 st each end of needle. **Next row,** with right side facing you, K 0 (1-1), P 5, K 5, P 5, K 0 (1-1). Keep pattern as now established for 5 (5-4) inches. End with right side row. Inc 1 st each end of needle on next row. With right side facing, work next row as follows: K1 (2-2), P 5, K 5, P 5, K 1 (2-2). Keep pattern as now established for 5 (5-4) inches. End with right side row. **Next row,** inc 1 st each end of needle. **Next row,** with right side facing, K 2 (3-3), P 5, K 5, P 5, K 2 (3-3). Keep pattern as established. Make 1 more inc on large size 19 (21-23) sts. Work even until sleeve measures 16½ (18-18½) inches, or desired length to underarm.
Armhole: Bind off 2 sts at beg of the next 2 rows. Work 2 rows even. Dec 1 st each end every other row until 5 (5-5) sts remain. Bind off.

■ **Finishing:** With right sides together and wrong side facing you, using 1 strand of French Floss weave side, sleeve, and raglan seams. Turn sweater right side out and reweave seams, keeping work flat. With No. J crochet hook and 3 strands of yarn, work 1 row sc around bottom, sleeve, and neck edge.

■ **Collar:** Using Reynolds Junior Jumbo Jet knitting needles and 3 strands of yarn (1 of each kind) cast on 50 sts. Work in pattern of K 5 sts, P 5 sts, across row. Repeat this row until 13 inches in all. Bind off in ribbing.

■ **Finishing:** Using 1 strand of French Floss, weave seam on wrong side. Turn right side out and reweave, keeping seam flat. Using No. J crochet hook and 3 strands of yarn, work 1 row sc around both edges of collar. Collar may be attached to back of neck and used as a hood if you wish.

Ribbed Sweater

Twisted Stockinette Sweater

Twisted Stockinette Sweater

- **Sizes:** Directions are written for small size (8-10). Changes for medium size (12-14) and large size (16-18) are in parentheses.

- **Materials: Reynolds Kirsti** 2 (3-3) balls; **French Floss 3 (4-4) balls; Danskyarn** 3 (4-4) balls and **Mohair No. 1,** 2 (3-3) balls.

- **Knitting Needles Required:** 1 pair **Reynolds Jumbo Jets.** Aluminum crochet hook size J. Two ping-pong balls for collar trim.

- **IMPORTANT:** Before starting garment, see Helpful Hints and Sizing.

- **Gauge:** 7 sts = 5"; 5 rows = 3".

- **Pattern:** Twisted Stockinette Stitch—knit into back of each st on knit row. Purl as usual.

- **Back:** Using Reynolds Jumbo Jet knitting needles and 5 strands of yarn (1 of Kirsti, Danskyarn and Mohair No. 1, and 2 of French Floss) cast on 22 (24-26) sts. Work even in twisted stockinette st until 16 (17-17½) inches or desired length to underarm.
Armholes: Bind off 2 (2-2) sts at beg of the next 2 rows. Dec 1 st each end every other row until 8 (10-10) sts remain. Bind off.

- **Front:** Work same as Back to underarm.
Armholes: Bind off 2 (2-2) sts at beg of the next 2 rows. Dec 1 st each end every other row until 10 (12-12) sts remain. Bind off.

- **Sleeves:** Using Reynolds Jumbo Jet knitting needles and 5 strands of yarn (same combination) cast on 14 (16-16) sts. Work in twisted stockinette st. Increase 1 st each end every 11 (11-7) rows until 16 (18-20) sts. Work even until sleeve measures 16 (17-17½)" or desired length to underarm.
Armholes: Bind off 2 (2-2) sts at beg of the next 2 rows. On small size only work 2 rows even. All sizes, dec 1 st each end every other row until 4 (4-4) sts remain. Bind off.

- **Collar:** Using Reynolds Jumbo Jet knitting needles and 5 strands of yarn (same combination) cast on 45 sts all sizes. Work even in stockinette st (purl side is right side) for 6 rows. Bind off loosely.

- **Finishing:** With right sides together and wrong side facing you, using 1 strand of French Floss weave side, sleeve, and raglan seams. Turn sweater right side out and reweave seams, keeping work flat. Fold collar in half lengthwise with purl side out, and weave seam from right side. Weave ends together to fold and fasten off. Attach ping-pong ball, covered (see Abbreviations and General Information), to each end of collar at the fold (see picture). Using No. J crochet hook and 5 strands of yarn, work 1 row sc around bottom of sweater and sleeves and around neck edge. Collar may be attached to back of neck edge or left free and just tied.

Knit and Purl Striped Sweater

- **Sizes:** Directions are written for small size (8-10). Changes for medium size (12-14) and large size (16-18) are in parentheses.
- **Materials: Reynolds Malibu** 3 (3-4) balls; **Mohair No. 1,** 2 (3-3) balls; **French Floss** 2 (2-2) balls; **Versailles** 2 (2-3) balls.
- **Knitting Needles Required:** 1 pair **Reynolds Jumbo Jets.** Aluminum crochet hook size J.
- **Gauge:** 6 sts = 5"; 5 rows = 3".
- **Back:** Using Reynolds Jumbo Jet knitting needles and 4 strands of yarn (1 of each kind) cast on 18 (20-22) sts. Starting with a purl row, work in stockinette st (purl side is right side) until there are 6 purl "bumps" on right side. (End with a knit row.) Knit the next row to reverse pattern. Continue in stockinette st with knit side as right side for 5 rows. Knit next row to reverse pattern and work stockinette st for 5 rows. (Purl side is right side.) Continue to reverse the pattern every 5 rows until there are 3 purl bands. Work should measure about 16". If you want your sweater longer or shorter do more or less rows to underarm, but be sure to reverse pattern every 5 rows in any case.
Armhole: Bind off 2 (2-2) sts at beg of the next 2 rows. Continuing to reverse pattern every 5 rows, dec 1 st each end every other row until 8 (8-10) sts remain. Bind off.
- **Front:** Using Reynolds Jumbo Jet knitting needles and 4 strands of yarn (1 of each kind) work same as Back to underarm. Start underarm on same row that you used for Back.
Armhole: Bind off 2 (2-2) sts at beg of the next 2 rows. Work 2 (0-2) rows even. Dec 1 st each end every other row until 10 (10-12) sts remain. Bind off.
- **Sleeves:** Using Reynolds Jumbo Jet knitting needles and 4 strands of yarn (1 of each kind) cast on 14 (16-18) sts. Work same as Back, being sure to reverse pattern every 5 rows, until there are 3 purl bands. Work will measure about 16". If you have started the armhole on the body of the sweater with more or less rows, start sleeve armhole on same row of pattern.
Armhole: Bind off 2 (2-2) sts at beg of the next 2 rows. Dec 1 st each end every other row until 4 (6-6) sts remain. Bind off.
- **Finishing:** With right sides together (the purl band on bottom is right side) and wrong side facing you, using 1 strand of French Floss, weave side, sleeve and raglan seams. Turn work right side out and reweave seams, keeping work flat. Using No. J crochet hook and 4 strands of yarn, work 1 row sc around bottom, sleeve, and neck edges.

Knit and Purl Striped Sweater

Triple Treat

- **Sizes:** Directions are for small size (8-10). Changes for medium size (12-14) and large size (16-18) are in parentheses.

- **Materials:** 1 pr. **Reynolds Jumbo Jet** Knitting Needles. 1 #K aluminum crochet hook.
Shrimp Color Combination: #1004 **Place Concorde** 7 (7-8) balls; #512 **Versailles** 5 (5-6) balls; #1709 **Monique** 5 (5-6) balls; **Orange Sherbert Super Cabri** 4 (4-5) balls.
Note: Use 1 strand each of **Place Concorde, Monique** and **Super Cabri.** Use **2 strands** of **Versailles.**
Aqua: #1012 **Place Concorde** 7 (7-8) balls; #541 **Versailles** 5 (5-6) balls; #1709 **Monique** 5 (5-6) balls; #85 **Torquoise-Super Cabri** 4 (4-5) balls.
Note: Use 1 strand each of **Place Concorde, Monique** and **Super Cabri.** Use **2 strands** of **Versailles.**
Pink Mauve: #690 **Plumage** 7 (7-8) balls; #535 **Versailles** 5 (5-6) balls; #1710 **Monique** 5 (5-6) balls; **Azalée Super Cabri** 4 (4-5)balls.
Note: Use **1 Monique**—1 **Plumage**—1 **Super Cabri.** Use **2 strands** of **Versailles.**

- **Gauge:** 3 sts = 3"; 3 rows = 2".

- **Back:** With Reynolds Jumbo Jet Knitting Needles and **5** strands of yarn, cast on 18 (20-22) sts; work even in stockinette for 17 (17½-17½)" or desired length to underarm.
Armholes: Bind off 2 (2-2) sts at beg of next 2 rows. Decrease 1 st each end of needle every 3rd row until 6 (8-8) sts remain. Bind off.

- **Front:** Work same as back to armhole.
Armholes: Bind off 2 (2-2) sts at beg of next 2 rows. Decrease 1 st each end of needle every **3rd row** until 8 (10-10) sts remain. Bind off.

- **Sleeves:** With Jumbo Jets and **5** strands of yarn, cast on 18 (20-22) sts.* Work even in stockinette for 8 (10-10) rows. Decrease 1 st each end of needle. Repeat from *. Work even for 5 rows.
- **Raglan Armhole Shaping:** Bind off 2 sts at beg of next 2 rows. Decrease 1 st each end of needle every **3rd** row until 4 (6-8) sts remain. Bind off.

- **Finishing:** With front and back pieces inside out, sew from "bump to

Triple Treat

bump" or "notch to notch" with 1 strand of Versailles. Sew sleeve seams in like manner. Sew in sleeves and ease raglan shaping. Turn sweater to right side and weave sts at each side of seam together. Pull yarn snugly making seam almost disappear. Do same at sleeve and raglan seams. With #K Aluminum Crochet Hook and 5 strands of yarn, pull a loop through, and (working on right side of finished garment) chain stitch loosely through sweater just above sleeve edge to make border. Tie off. Repeat on other sleeve, neck edge, and hem of sweater.

■ **Triangle Headscarf:** With 5 strands of yarn, cast on 18 sts. Stockinette for 4 rows. Dec 1 st each end of needle on next row, then every 3rd row twice. Continue to dec 1 st each end **every** row until 2 sts remain. Work 2 sts tog, fasten off.

■ **Ties:** With 5 strands of yarn and #K crochet hook, ch 27″ (make 2). Sew to front corners of triangle for chin ties. With 5 strands of yarn, in same manner as on sweater, pull loop through with crochet hook; working inside edges of triangle, ch st around evenly.

Rich Boy Sweater

■ **Sizes:** Directions are for small size (8-10). Changes for medium size (12-14) and large size (16-18) are in parentheses.

■ **Materials:** 1 pr. **Reynolds Jumbo Jet** Knitting Needles. 1 #J Aluminum Crochet Hook, 2 ping-pong balls (for hat).

Note: The Rich Boy costume is made up of 4 separate pieces. 1) Sweater. 2) Large separate stand-up collar. (This is also worn lying flat in a petal effect). 3) Hat with drawstring top. 4) Rolled brim for hat which also doubles as a snug fitting turtle neck collar for sweater.

Sweater: 14 (16-18) balls #1701 **Monique;** 3 (3-3) balls **White No. 1 Mohair.**

Large Collar: 5 (5-5) balls **Monique;** 1 (1-1) ball **Super Cabri.**

Hat: 3 (3-3) balls **Monique;** 1 (1-1) ball **Super Cabri.**

Hat Brim: 3 (3-3) balls **Monique;** 1 (1-1) ball **Super Cabri.** If knitter plans to make complete costume (4 pieces), subtract 3 Monique and 1 No. 1 Mohair from total amount needed for all sizes.

Use 3 strands of **Monique** and 1 strand of **Super Cabri** for all pieces, (every size).

■ **Gauge:** Stockinette: 3 sts = 3"; 5 rows = 3". Make test piece in stockinette for sizing (see rules at beg of book). The K 1, P 1 ribbing will appear looser but judge size by stockinette gauge.

■ **Back:** With Jumbo Jet Knitting Needles and 3 strands of Monique plus 1 strand of No. 1 Mohair, cast on 18 (20-22) sts. Work even in K 1, P 1 ribbing for 20 (22-22) rows. Change to stockinette stitch and work even until piece measures 17 (18-18)", or desired length to underarm.

Armhole: Bind off 2 (2-2) sts at beg of next 2 rows. Work 1 more row even. Dec 1 st each end of needle every other row until 6 (8-8) sts remain. Bind off.

■ **Front:** Work the same as back to armhole.

Armhole: Bind off 2 (2-2) sts at beg of next 2 rows. Work 1 more row even. Dec 1 st each end of needle every row until 8 (10-10) sts remain. Bind off.

■ **Sleeve:** With Jumbo Jet Needles and 4 strands of yarn, cast on 12 (12-14) sts. Work even in K 1, P 1 ribbing for 10 (12-12) rows. **Next Row:** Change to stockinette st, increasing 1 st each end of needle on that first row. Continue in stockinette increasing 1 st each end of needle every fourth row until 16 (16-18) sts and 17" from beg (or desired length to underarm).

Armhole: Bind off 2 sts at beg of next 2 rows. Work 1 row even. Decrease 1 st each end of needle every other row until 4 (4-6) remain. Bind off.

■ **Finishing:** Turn body pieces inside out. Sew together "bump to bump" or "notch to notch" with Monique yarn which you have split to half thickness. Sew sleeve seams in same manner, matching side and underarm seams; ease in raglan. (Front is slightly lower, ease in evenly). Turn sweater to right side. With split strand of Monique, weave seams together matching stitch for stitch so that seams will almost disappear. Do this on side seams, sleeve seams, and finally pull raglan seams together in this manner. Avoid bunching.

With #J Crochet Hook and 2 strands of Monique and 1 strand of Super Cabri sc around neck edge neatly.

■ **Large Collar:** With Jumbo Jet Knitting Needles and 4 strands of yarn,

Rich Boy Sweater

cast on 38 (40-40) sts. Work even in K 1, P 1 ribbing for 16 (18-18) rows. Bind off. Join ends and sew together to form ring with split strand of Monique. Fold over and sew or crochet 2 edges of ring together. **Note:** For permanent collar sew 1 edge to sweater, fold over; or, for stand-up collar, make single strand Monique ch with #J crochet hook. Weave in and out at top fold of ribbing; pull collar as snug as you wish; tie in adjustable bow knot on inside.

■ **Hat:** With Jumbo Jet Knitting Needles and 4 strands of yarn cast on 20 sts (all sizes). K 1, P 1 for 18 rows. Don't bind off. Leaving 10" strands of 4 yarns, remove piece from needle and draw strands through and secure after pulling tightly.

Tie for top of hat: With 3 strands of Monique, and #J Aluminum Crochet Hook chain 58". Weave in ends. Sew side edges together. Pull together with weaving stitch as on sweater seams. Pull 58" sc streamer through top loops (to be tied in loopy bow).

Covered ping-pong ball bubbles for streamer ends are optional. With one strand of Monique cover 2 ping-pong balls with crochet (see General Information). Sew to end of chain.

Hat Brim (Also used as small collar): With Jumbo Jet Knitting Needles and 4 strands of yarn, cast on 30 sts. Work even in K 1, P 1 ribbing for 14 rows. Bind off. Join ends and sew together to form ring with split strand of Monique. Fold over and sew or crochet 2 edges of ring together.

Purl Stripe

- **Sizes:** Directions are for misses' size 8-10. Changes for sizes 12-14 and 16-18 are in parentheses. Pullover fits bust size 28-30" (32-34"; 36-38").

- **Materials:** Reynolds **Monique,** 6 (7-8) balls Main color (MC) and 6 (7-8) balls white; Reynolds **Super Cabri,** 4 (4-5) balls white; **Reynolds Scotch Mist,** 4 (4-5) balls (see color combinations). **Reynolds Jumbo Jet** Knitting Needles. Aluminum crochet hook size J. One ping pong ball for button on collar.

- **Note:** Pullover worked with 4 strands held together (2 Monique, 1 each of Super Cabri and Scotch Mist).

- **Gauge:** 4 sts = 3"; 6 rows = 3½".

- **Pattern: Purl Stripe: Rows 1-5:** Beg right side, p 1 row, k 1 row alternately.

- **Knit Stripe: Row 6-10:** Beg wrong side, p 1 row, k 1 row alternately. Repeat these 10 rows for striped pat.

- **Back:** With 1 strand of each color, cast on evenly 18 (20-22) sts. K 1 row in back loop of sts. Work in striped pat until 3 purl stripes are completed.
- **Shape Sleeves:** Keeping in pat, cast on 5 (7-7) sts at beg of next 2 rows, 5 sts at beg of next 4 rows—48 (54-56) sts. Work even for 3 (3-5) rows.
- **Shape Back Neck:** Work first 21 (24-24) sts, sl these sts on st holder; bind off next 6 (6-8) sts for neck, finish row. Work even on left shoulder for 3 (5-5) rows, ending at neck edge. Place these 21 (24-24) sts on st holder.
- **Right Shoulder:** Place sts from holder on needle, join yarn at neck edge and work even for 3 (5-5) rows, ending at sleeve edge.

- **Front: Next Row:** Work to neck edge, cast on 6 (6-8) sts for front neck; beg at neck edge, work sts of left shoulder—48 (54-56) sts. Work even for 4 (4-6) rows. Bind off 5 sts at beg of next 4 rows, 5 (7-7) sts at beg of next 2 rows—18 (20-22) sts. Work in striped pat until 3 purl stripes are completed as on back below sleeves. K 1 row. Bind off in purl same tension as sts.

- **Finishing:** DO NOT STEAM OR BLOCK PULLOVER. With split length

84

of MC Monique and garment inside out, weave side and sleeve seams from "bump to bump" with loose tension and matching stripes. Turn pullover to right side. Weave seams tog again with zigzag stitches, catching edge on either side of seams and drawing tog evenly (seams almost disappear). Right side facing, with 1 strand of each color, work 1 row sc around neck and sleeve edges.

■ **Collar or Headband:** With 1 strand of each color, cast on evenly 22 sts. Work in stockinette st (k 1 row, p 1 row) for 9 rows. Bind off.

■ **Button:** With 1 strand MC and crochet hook, ch 4. Join with sl st to form ring. **Rnd 1:** 8 sc in ring. **Rnds 2 and 3:** Sc in each sc around. **Rnd 4:** Place over ping-pong ball, sc in every other sc on rnd. End off, leaving yarn to sew with. Pull end through sts; draw sts tog. End off. Using purl side for right side of collar, sew button to one short end of collar. With same yarn as buttons, make crocheted buttonloop on other end of collar opposite button.

Purl Stripe

Military

■ **Sizes:** Directions are for small size (8-10). Changes for medium size (12-14) and large size (16-18) are in parentheses.

■ **Fits Bust Size:** 28-30 (32-34; 36-38)".

■ **Materials: Reynolds** white **Monique (A)** 5 (6-6) balls; **one other color** (navy, green or black) **Monique (B)** 6 (7-7) balls; red **Monique** (C) 3 (4-4) balls; white **French Floss (D)** 2 (3-3) balls; **Chanson de Paris** 3 (4-4) balls **or Versailles (E)** 3 (3-4) balls to match Monique (B) (navy, green or black).

■ **Knitting needles required:** 1 pair **Reynolds Jumbo Jets; Jumbo Jet Hook.** Aluminum crochet hook size J. 4 ping-pong balls for trim. Buckram hat shape as pictured.

■ **IMPORTANT:** Before starting dress, see Helpful Hints and Sizing.

■ **Gauge:** 6 sts = 5½"; 3 rows = 2". Make test piece in stockinette st for sizing (see Helpful Hints, No. 2). Rip and re-use test piece.

■ **Note:** White braids of trim are crocheted and sewn on later.

■ **Back:** With 1 strand each of A, B, D and E (4) held tog, cast on 18 (20-22) sts. Work even in stockinette st for 17½ (18-18½)". Keep track of rows worked.
■ **Raglan Armholes:** Bind off 2 sts at beg of next 2 rows. Dec 1 st each edge every 3rd row 3 (2-4) times, every other row 0 (2-0) times, work 1 (1-0) row even. Bind off remaining 8 (8-10) sts.

■ **Front:** Work same as back to underarms.
■ **Raglan Armholes:** Bind off 2 sts at beg of next 2 rows. Dec 1 st each edge every 3rd row 2 (3-3) times, work 2 (0-1) rows even. Bind off remaining 10 (10-12) sts.

■ **Sleeves:** Using 3 strands of C Monique, cast on 8 (10-12) sts. Work in reverse stockinette st (p 1 row [right side], k 1 row) for 9 rows, ending with a p row. Inc 1 st each edge on next k row. Work even for 3 rows more, ending with a p row. Break off C. With 3 strands B Monique: p 3 rows, k 2 rows. Break off B. With same 4 strands as for back, work in stockinette st (k 1 row on right side, p 1 row) hereafter, inc 1 st each edge on first row. Work even on 12 (14-16) sts until total length is 17 (17½-17½)".

■ **Raglan Cap:** Bind off 2 sts at beg of next 2 rows. Dec 1st each edge every 3rd row 2 (2-3) times—4 (6-6) sts. Work even for 2 (2-1) rows. Bind off 2 (2-3) sts at beg of k rows 2 (3-2) times for right sleeve; beg of p rows for left sleeve.

Military

■ **Finishing:** DO NOT STEAM OR BLOCK. With 1 strand French Floss or ½ strand Monique in matching color, sew raglan seams, side and sleeve seams (see General Information). With 4 strands to match body and Jumbo Jet hook, work 1 row sc loosely around neck, 1 row sc and 1 row sl st loosely around lower edge. With 3 strands White Monique and Jumbo Jet hook make 2 crocheted chains to fit around center of dark stripe on sleeves; join with sl st in first chain to form ring. Fasten off and sew to sleeves.

■ **Collar:** With 3 strands of C Monique cast on 21 (22-23) sts. (K 1 row, p 1 row) twice. Break off C. With 3 strands B Monique, P 3 rows, k 2 rows, bind off. Make a chain same as for sleeve to fit around collar. With 1 strand C Monique cover 2 ping-pong balls (see General Information), and make a chain to fit around it for buttonloop; another buttonloop with B Monique. Sew a matching buttonloop to each corner on one end of collar, ping-pons on opposite corners.

■ **Hat: Top Section:** Use 1 strand B Monique and J hook. Wrap strand around one finger to form a .ring. Insert hook in ring and pull up a loop. **Rnd 1:** Make 6 sc in ring. **Mark last sc on each rnd for accurate shaping and work in back loop only of each sc. Rnd 2:** 2 sc in each sc (12 sc). **Rnd 3:** * Sc in next sc, 2 sc in next sc. Repeat from * around (18 sc). **Rnd 4:** * 2 sc in next sc, sc in next 2 sc. Repeat from * around (24 sc). **Rnd 5:** Make 2 sc in every 4th sc (30 sc). **Rnd 6:** 2 sc in every 5th sc (36 sc). **Rnd 7:** Sc in each sc. Fasten off.

■ **Side Piece:** With 4 yarns to match body of sweater, cast on 25 sts. Work even in stockinette st, decreasing 1 st each edge every 3rd row twice, work 2 rows even on 21 sts. Bind off, sew edges tog. Pin last rnd of top to last row of side piece, wrong sides together. With same 4 strands, Jumbo Jet hook and side piece toward you, join edges with 1 row sl st. Pull this section over buckram crown and sew to back edge.

■ **Visor:** Starting at upper edge with 1 B to match top and J hook, ch 22. **Row 1:** Sc in 2nd ch from hook and each ch across (21 sc). **Row 2-6:** Skip first sc, sc in each st to within last sc (2 sc decreased); 11 sc remain on Row 6. Fasten off. Fold piece in half, sew curved edge to upper edge of visor; tack upper edge to side piece. With 3 strands white Monique and Jumbo Jet hook, make chain to fit across top of visor, sew in place. With 3rd color Monique cover 2 ping-pong balls (see General Information) and sew to corners of visor. With 3 strands B Monique and Jumbo Jet hook, make a chain 16″ long for chin-strap and sew ends under buckram on each side behind visor.

Woman's Fisherman Sweater

Woman's Fisherman Sweater

■ **Sizes:** Directions are written in small size (8-10). Changes for medium size (12-14) and large size (16-18) are in parentheses.

■ **Materials:** 1 pair **Reynolds Jr. Jumbo Jet** knitting needles. #4447 scoured **Irish Fisherman** yarn 14 skeins. 1 #K aluminum crochet hook. 1 spare DP needle or cable needle.

■ **Gauge:** 5 sts = 3″; 5 rows = 2″.

■ **PATTERN STITCHES**

■ **Twisted Rib: Row 1:** K 1 in back of st, P 1 repeat across row. **Row 2:** P 1 in back of st. K 1 repeat across. Repeat these 2 rows for pattern.

- **Seed St: Row 1:** K 1, p 1 across row. **Row 2:** P over the k st and k over the p st. Repeat row 2 for pattern.

- **Cable St** (6 sts): **Row 1:** P 1, k 4, p 1. **Row 2:** K 1, p 4, k 1. **Row 3:** P 1, sl 1 to DP needle and hold in back of work, k 1 from left needle, k 1 from DP needle; sl 1 to DP needle and hold in front of work, k 1 from left needle, k 1 from DP needle, p 1. **Row 4:** K 1, p 4, k 1. Repeat rows 3 and 4 for pattern st.

- **Popcorn Diamond** (9 sts): **Row 1:** P 3, k 1b (knit into back of st), p 1, k 1b, p 3. **Row 2:** K 3, p 1b (purl into back of st), k 1, p 1b, k 3. **Row 3:** P 2, sl 1 to DP needle and hold in back of work, k 1b from left needle, p st on DP needle (right cross made), p 1; sl 1 to DP needle and hold in front of work, p 1 from left needle, k 1b from DP needle (left cross made), p 2. **Row 4:** K 2, p 1b, k 3, p 1b, k 2. **Row 5:** p 1, right cross, p 3, left cross, p 1. **Row 6:** K 1, p 1b, k 5, p 1b, k 1. **Row 7:** right cross, p 1; (k, p, k) into next st to make a popcorn, k next st and turn, p 3 and turn, sl 2nd and 3rd st over first st and p into back of first st, p 2, left cross. **Row 8:** P 1b, k 7, p 1b. **Row 9:** Left cross, p 5, right cross. **Row 10:** K 1, p 1b, k 5, p 1b, k 1. **Row 11:** P 1, left cross, p 3, right cross, p 1. **Row 12:** K 2, p 1b, k 3, p 1b, k 2. **Row 13:** P 2, left cross, p 1, right cross, p 2.

Row 14: K 3, p 1b, k 1, p 1b, k 3. **Row 15:** P 3, sl next 2 sts to DP needle and hold in back of work, k 1b from left needle, k 1b from DP needle, p 1 from DP needle, p 3. **Row 16:** K 4, p 2b, k 3. **Row 17:** P 3, k 1b, left cross, P 3. Repeat rows 2-17 for pattern.

- **Back:** Using Reynolds Jr. Jumbo Jet knitting needles and 3 strands of yarn cast on 29 (31-33) sts. Work 8 rows in twisted rib pattern. Starting with p 1 for row 1 on sizes small and large, and k 1 for row 2 on same sizes, set up pattern for body of sweater as follows. Work 4 (5-6) sts in seed st, 6 sts in Cable, 9 sts in popcorn diamond, 6 sts in cable, 4 (5-6) sts in seed st. Work in patterns as established until 16½ (17½-18½)" or desired length to underarm.
- **Armhole:** Bind off 2 (2-2) sts at beg of the next 2 rows. Dec 1 st each end every other row until 9 (11-11) sts remain. Bind off.

- **Front:** Work same as to back underarm. Bind off 2 (2-2) sts at beg of the next 2 rows. Dec 1 st each end until 11 (13-13) sts remain. Bind off.

- **Sleeves:** Using Jr. Jumbo Jet knitting needles and 3 strands of yarn, cast on 15 (15-17) sts. Work 8 rows in twisted rib pattern, starting with p 1 for row 1 on large size only, and k 1 for row 2, on same size. Inc 1 st each end of needle on 8th row and every 8 (8-8)th row until there are 21 (21-23) sts. After the 1st inc row (end of twisted rib pattern), set up pattern as follows. Work 3 (3-4) sts in seed, p 1, 9 sts in popcorn diamond, p 1, 3 (3-4) sts seed. Working all increased sts in seed st, keeping pattern as established, work until sleeve measures 16½ (17½-18½)", or desired length to underarm.
- **Armhole:** Bind off 1 (1-1) st at beg of the next 2 rows. Work 2 rows even. Dec 1 st each end every other row until 5 (5-5) sts remain. Bind off.

- **Collar:** Using Jr. Jumbo Jet knitting needles and 3 strands of yarn, cast on 36 sts. Work rib pattern as follows for 3 inches. **Row 1:** K 1 in back of st, p 1, repeat across. **Row 2:** K 1, p 1 across. Bind off in ribbing.

- **Finishing:** With right sides together, wrong side facing you, using 1 strand of yarn, weave side, sleeve and raglan seams. Turn work right side out and reweave seams. Keep work flat. Weave short ends of collar tog and sew collar around neck edge loosely, having right side of collar facing wrong side of sweater so it will turn over in a modified turtle neck. Using #K crochet hook and 3 strands of yarn, work 1 row sc around bottom of sweater and sleeves; this crocheting is optional.

Daughter's Fisherman Sweater

▪ **Sizes:** Directions are written for size (8). Changes for size (10) and size (12) are in parentheses.

▪ **Materials:** 1 pair **Reynolds Jr. Jumbo Jet** knitting needles. #4447 Irish Fisherman yarn (10). 1 #K aluminum crochet hook. 1 spare DP needle or cable needle.

▪ **Gauge:** 5 sts = 3"; 5 rows = 2".

▪ **PATTERN STITCHES.**

▪ **Twisted Rib: Row 1:** K 1 in back of st, p 1, repeat across row. **Row 2:** P 1 in back of st, k 1 repeat across row. Repeat these 2 rows for pattern.

▪ **Seed St: Row 1:** K 1, p 1, across row. **Row 2:** P over the k st and k over the p st. Repeat row 2 for pattern.

▪ **Cable St** (6 sts): **Row 1:** P 1, k 4, p 1. **Row 2:** K 1, p 4, k 1. **Row 3:** P 1, sl 1 to DP needle and hold in back of work, k 1 from left needle, k 1 from DP needle, sl 1 to DP needle and hold in front of work, k 1 from left needle, k 1 from DP needle, p 1. **Row 4:** K 1, p 4, k 1. Repeat rows 3 and 4 for pattern.

▪ **Popcorn Diamond** (9 sts): **Row 1:** P 3, k lb (knit into back of st), p 1, k lb, p 3. **Row 2:** K 3, p lb (purl into back of st), k 1, p lb, k 3. **Row 3:** P 2, sl 1 to DP needle and hold in back of work, k lb from left needle. P 1 from DP needle (right cross made), p 1, sl 1 to DP needle and hold in front of work, p 1 from left needle, k lb from DP needle (left cross made), p 2. **Row 4:** K 2, p lb, k 3, p lb, k 2. **Row 5:** p 1, right cross, p 3, left cross, p 1. **Row 6:** K 1, p lb, k 5, p lb, k 1. **Row 7:** right cross, p 1, k, p, k into next st to make a popcorn, k next st and turn, p 3 and turn, sl 2nd and 3rd sts over first st and p into back of first st, p 2, left cross. **Row 8:** P lb, k 7, p lb. **Row 9:** Left cross, p 5, right cross. **Row 10:** K 1, p lb, k 5, p lb, k 1. **Row 11:** P 1, left cross, p 3, right cross, p 1. **Row 12:** K 2, p lb, k 3, p lb, k 2. **Row 13:** P 2, left cross, p 1, right cross, p 2. **Row 14:** K 3, p lb, k 1, p lb, k 3. **Row 15:** P 3, sl next 2 sts to DP needle and hold in back of work, k lb from left needle, k lb from DP needle, p 1 from DP needle, p 3. **Row 16:** K 4, p 2b, k 3. **Row 17:** P 3, k lb, left cross, p 3. Repeat rows 2-17 for pattern.

■ **Back:** Using Reynolds Jr. Jumbo Jet knitting needles and 3 strands of yarn, cast on 23 (25-27) sts. Work in twisted rib pattern for 6 rows, starting with p 1 for row 1 on medium size, and k 1 for row 2 on same size. Set up pattern for body of sweater as follows. Work 1 (2-3) seed, 6 sts cable, 9 sts popcorn diamond, 6 sts cable, and 1 (2-3) sts seed. Keeping patterns as established, work until 13½ (14½-15½)", or desired length to underarm.

■ **Armhole:** Bind off 2 (2-2) sts at beg of the next 2 rows. Dec 1 st each end every other row until 5 (5-7) sts remain.

■ **Front:** Work same as back to underarm. Bind off 2 (2-2) sts at beg of the next 2 rows. Dec 1 st each end every other row until 7 (7-9) sts remain. Bind off.

■ **Sleeve:** Using Jr. Jumbo Jet knitting needles and 3 strands of yarn cast on 11 (13-13) sts. Work 6 rows in twisted rib st. Start with p 1 for row 1 on medium and large sizes, and k 1 for row 2 on same sizes. Next row set up pattern as follows. Work 1 (2-2) sts seed, 9 sts diamond, 1 (2-2) sts seed. Next row inc 1 st each end of needle all sizes keeping pattern as established and all inc st in seed st, inc 1 st each end every 5 (6-7)th row until 17 (19-19) sts. Work even until sleeve measures 12½ (13½-15)" or desired length to underarm.

■ **Armhole:** Bind off 1 (1-1) st at beg of the next 2 rows. Work 2 rows even. Dec 1 st each end every other row until 3 (3-3) sts remain. Bind off.

■ **Collar:** Using Jr. Jumbo Jet knitting needles and 3 strands of yarn cast on 30 sts. Work in ribbing as follows for 3". **Row 1:** K 1 in back of st p 1, repeat across. **Row 2:** K 1, p 1 across row. Repeat these two rows. Bind off.

■ **Finishing:** With right sides together, wrong side facing you, weave side, sleeve and raglan seams, using 1 strand of yarn. Turn sweater right side out and reweave seams, keeping work flat. Join short ends of collar, having right side of collar against wrong side of sweater. Attach collar around neck edges; turn collar over to form a modified turtle neck line. If desired work 1 row sc around bottom of sweater and sleeves. Use #K crochet hook and 3 strands of yarn.

Sweaters for Men and Boys

Fisherman's Sweater for Boys

■ **Sizes:** Directions are for small size (8). Changes for medium size (10) and large size (12) are in parentheses.

■ **Materials: Reynolds Malibu** 2 (2-2) balls color A, **Monique** 3 (4-4) balls color B, **Monique** 3 (4-4) balls color C. This sweater may be made in any 3 colors of these 2 yarns you choose to combine.

■ **Knitting Needles Required: Reynolds Junior Jumbo Jets.** Aluminum crochet hook size K.

■ **Gauge:** 3 sts = 2"; 2 rows = 1".

■ **Back:** With Junior Jumbo Jet knitting needles and 3 strands of yarn (1 strand of each color), cast on 20 (22-24) sts. Work even in stockinette st, using purl side as right side, until piece measures 10 (10½-11)" or desired length to underarm. End with a knit row.

■ **Armhole:** Bind off 2 (2-2) sts at the beginning of the next 2 rows. Dec 1 st each end every other row until 4 (6-6) sts remain. Bind off.

■ **Front:** With Junior Jumbo Jet knitting needles and 3 strands of yarn, cast on 20 (22-24) sts. Work in pattern as follows:
Row 1: P 6 (7-8), K 1, P 1, K 4, P 1, K 1, P 6 (7-8). **Row 2:** K 6 (7-8), P 1, K 1, P 4, K 1, P 1, K 6 (7-8). **Row 3:** P 6 (7-8), K 1, P 1, K 4, P 1, K 1, P 6 (7-8). **Row 4:** K 6 (7-8), P 1, K 1, P 4, K 1, P 1, K 6 (7-8). **Row 5:** P 6 (7-8), K 1, P 1, turn cable on next 4 sts as follows: slip next 2 sts to crochet hook and hold in back of work, knit next 2 sts from left needle, knit the 2 sts from crochet hook. P 1, K 1, P 6 (7-8). * **Row 6:** K 6 (7-8), P 1, K 1, P 4, K 1, P 1, K 6 (7-8). **Row 7:** P 6 (7-8), K 1, P 1, K 4, P 1, K 1, P 6 (7-8). **Row 8:** K 6 (7-8), P 1, K 1, P 4, K 1, P 1, K 6 (7-8). **Row 9:** P 6 (7-8), K 1, P 1, K 4, P 1, K 1, P 6 (7-8). **Row 10:** K 6 (7-8), P 1, K 1, P 4, K 1, P 1, K 6 (7-8). **Row 11:** P 6 (7-8), K 1, P 1, turn cable on next 4 sts. P 1, K 1, P 6 (7-8).
Repeat from * until piece measures 10 (10½-11)" or desired length to underarm. Continue in pattern.

■ **Armhole:** Bind off 2 (2-2) sts at beg of the next 2 rows. Dec 1 st each end of needle every other row until 6 (8-8) sts remain. Bind off.

■ **Sleeves:** With Junior Jumbo Jet knitting needles and 3 strands of yarn, cast on 10 (12-14) sts. Work even in stockinette st, using P side as right side, for 5 (5-5) rows. **Next row:** Increase 1 st each end of needle. Continue to inc 1 st each end of needle every 6th (6th-6th) row until 18 (20-22) sts are on needle. Work even until 14½ (15-16)" in all, or desired length to underarm.

■ **Armhole:** Bind off 2 (2-2) sts at beg of the next 2 rows. Dec 1 st each end of needle every other row until 4 (4-6) sts remain. Bind off.

Fisherman's Sweater for Men

■ **Finishing:** Place pieces of garment so knit sides are together and purl side (right side) faces you. With 1 strand of Monique **split** sew side seams and sleeves seams together, working "purl bumps" to correspond to each other. Set raglan sleeves in and ease raglan shaping. With #K aluminum crochet hook and 3 strands of yarn, sc around neck, sleeves and bottom of sweater.

Fisherman's Sweater for Men

- **Sizes:** Directions are for small size (36-38). Changes for medium size (40-42) and large size (44-46) are in parentheses.
- **Materials: Reynolds Malibu** 3 (4-4) balls color A, **Monique** 6 (7-7) balls color B, **Monique** 6 (7-7) balls color C. This sweater may be made in any 3 colors of these 2 yarns you choose to combine.
- **Knitting Needles Required: Reynolds Jumbo Jets.** Aluminum crochet hook size K.
- **Gauge:** 3 sts = 2½"; 2 rows = 1".
- **Back:** With Jumbo Jet knitting needles and 3 strands of yarn (1 strand of each color) cast on 20 (22-24) sts. Work even in stockinette st, using purl side as right side, for 16 (17-17½)" or desired length to underarm. End with a knit row.
- **Armhole:** Bind off 1 (1-1) st at the beg of next 2 rows. Dec 1 st each end of needle every other row until 4 (6-6) sts remain. Bind off.
- **Front:** With Jumbo Jet knitting needles and 3 strands of yarn (1 strand each color) cast on 20 (22-24) sts and work in pattern.
- **Pattern: Row 1:** P 6 (7-8), K 1, P 1, K 4, P 1, K 1, P 6 (7-8). **Row 2:** K 6 (7-8), P 1, K 1, P 4, K 1, P 1, K 6 (7-8). **Row 3:** P 6 (7-8), K 1, P 1, K 4, P 1, K 1, P 6 (7-8). **Row 4:** K 6 (7-8), P 1, K 1, P 4, K 1, P 1, K 6 (7-8). **Row 5:** P 6 (7-8), K 1, P 1, turn cable on next 4 sts as follows: slip next 2 sts to crochet hook, hold in back of work, knit next 2 sts from left needle, knit the 2 sts from crochet hook. P 1, K 1, P 6 (7-8). * **Row 6:** K 6 (7-8), P 1, K 1, P 4, K 1, P 1, K 6 (7-8). **Row 7:** P 6 (7-8), K 1, P 1, K 4, P 1, K 1, P 6 (7-8). **Row 8:** K 6 (7-8), P 1, K 1, P 4, K 1, P 1, K 6 (7-8). **Row 9:** P 6 (7-8), K 1, P 1, K 4, P 1, K 1, P 6 (7-8). **Row 10:** K 6 (7-8), P 1, K 1, P 4, K 1, P 1, K 6 (7-8). **Row 11:** P 6 (7-8), K 1, P 1, turn cable on next 4 sts,* P 1, K 1, P 6 (7-8). Repeat from * until piece measures 16 (17-17½)" or desired length to underarm. End with wrong side row.
- **Armhole:** Continue to work in pattern, bind off 1 (1-1) st at beg next 2 rows. Dec 1 st each end of needle every other row until 6 (8-8) sts remain. Bind off.
- **Sleeves:** With Jumbo Jet knitting needles and 3 strands of yarn (1 strand each color) cast on 10 (12-12) sts. Work even in stockinette st, using Purl side as right side for 6 (6-6) rows. **Next row:** inc 1 st each end of needle. Repeat inc every 4th (4th-4th) row 3 (3-4) times. 18 sts (20 sts-22 sts) are on needle. Work even until piece measures 17½ (18-19)" or desired length to underarm.
- **Armhole:** Bind off 1 (1-1) st at the beg of the next 2 rows. Dec 1 st each end of needle every other row until 4 (4-4) sts remain. Bind off.
- **Finishing:** Place pieces of garment so knit sides are together and purl side (right side) faces you. With 1 strand of Monique, split, sew seams together, working "purl bumps" so seam doesn't show. Sew side seams and sleeve seams in above manner first; then set raglan sleeves in, shaping the seam as you work. Using a #K crochet hook and 3 strands of yarn, sc around neck edge, sleeves, and bottom of sweater.

Yachting Sweater for Men

■ **Sizes:** Directions are for small size (36-38). Changes for medium size (40-42) and large size (44-46) are in parentheses.

■ **Materials: Reyonlds Monique** 4 (4-5) balls (A), **Monique** 3 (3-3) balls (B), **Pontresina** 8 (8-9) balls (A), **Pontresina** 4 (4-4) balls (B).

■ **Knitting Needles Required: Reynolds Jumbo Jets.** Aluminum crochet hook size K.

■ **Gauge:** 6 sts = 5"; 2 rows = 1".

■ **Back:** With Jumbo Jet knitting needles and 3 strands of A yarn (2 strands of A Pontresina and 1 strand of A Monique) cast on 22 (24-26) sts. Work even in stockinette st until piece measures 9 (10-11)". Be sure to end with a purl row. Break off A yarn. **Next row:** Join 3 strands of B yarn (2 strands of B Pontresina and 1 strand of B Monique) and knit across. Knit next row also (this will reverse the stockinette st so purl side of B yarn is right side). Work even in stockinette st until 9 (9-9) purl bumps are on right side. Piece should now measure 16 (17-18)".

■ **Armhole:** Bind off 2 (2-2) sts at the beginning of the next 2 rows. Break off B yarn. Join 3 strands of A yarn (2 strands of A Pontresina and 1 strand of A Monique) and knit this row, decreasing 1 st each end of needle. Continue working in stockinette st with knit side as right side, decreasing 1 st each end of needle every other row until 6 (6-6) sts remain. Bind off.

■ **Front:** Work same as back to underarm.

■ **Armhole:** Bind off 2 (2-2) sts at beginning of the next 2 rows. Break off B yarn. Join 3 strands of A yarn (2 strands of Pontresina and 1 strand of Monique) and knit this row, decreasing 1 st each end of needle. Continue working in stockinette st with knit side as right side, decreasing 1 st each end of needle every other row until 8 (8-8) sts remain. Bind off.

■ **Sleeves:** With Jumbo Jet knitting needles and 3 strands of A yarn (2 strands of Pontresina and 1 strand of Monique) cast on 10 (10-12) sts. Work even in stockinette st for 5 (5-5) rows. **Next row:** Inc 1 st each end of needle. Continue working in stockinette st, increasing 1 st each end of needle every 4th (4th-4th) row until 18 (20-22) sts are on needle. Work even in stockinette st until piece measures 10½ (11-11½)". Be sure to end with a purl row. Break off A yarn. Join 3 strands of B yarn (2 strands of Pontresina and 1 strand of Monique) and knit this row. **Next row:** Knit also. This will reverse the stockinette st so purl side of B yarn is right side. Work even in stockinette st until 9 (9-9) purl bumps are on

Yachting Sweater for Men

right side. Bind off 2 sts at beginning of the next 2 rows. Break off B yarn. Join 3 strands of A yarn and knit this row, decreasing 1 st each end of needle. Continue working in stockinette st with knit side as right side, decreasing 1 st each end of needle every other row until 4 (4-4) sts remain. Bind off.

■ **Finishing:** Place pieces of garment so knit sides are together and purl side faces you. With 1 split strand of Monique, sew side and sleeve seams "bump to bump." Leave B section open. Set sleeves in on wrong side. Turn sweater right side out and with split strand of Monique weave seams together on right side. With 1 split strand of B Monique sew purl "bumps" together on right side. With #K crochet hook and 3 strands of yarn, sc around bottom of sweater and sleeves; also neck edge.

■ **Note:** If sweater body or sleeves are to be lengthened or shortened, do so before joining B yarn.

Yachting Sweater for Boys

■ **Sizes:** Directions are for small size (8). Changes for medium size (10) and large size (12) are in parentheses.

■ **Materials: Reynolds Pontresina** 3 (3-4) balls (A), **Pontresina** 2 (2-2) balls (B), **Monique** 3 (3-4) balls (A), **Monique** 1 (1-1) ball (B).

■ **Knitting Needles Required: Reynolds Junior Jumbo Jets.** Aluminum crochet hook size K.

■ **Gauge:** 1½ sts = 1", 3 rows = 1".

■ **Back:** With Junior Jumbo Jet knitting needls and 3 strands of A yarn (2 strands A of Pontresina and 1 strand of A Monique) cast on 20 (22-24) sts. Work even in stockinette st until piece measures 8 (9-10)". Be sure to end with a purl row. Break off A yarn. Join 3 strands of B yarn (2 strands of B Pontresina and 1 strand of B Monique) and knit this row. Knit next row also. (This will reverse the stockinette st so purl side of B yarn is right side.) Work even in stockinette st until 9 (9-9) purl bumps are on right side. Piece should measure 12½ (13½-14½)".

■ **Armhole:** Bind off 2 (2-2) sts at beginning of the next 2 rows. Break off B yarn. Join 3 strands of A yarn (2 strands of A Pontresina and 1 strand of A Monique) and knit this row, decreasing 1 st each end of needle. Continue working in stockinette st, with knit side as right side, decreasing 1 st each end of needle every other row until 6 (6-6) sts remain. Bind off.

■ **Front:** Work same as back to underarm.

■ **Armhole:** Bind off 2 (2-2) sts at beginning of the next 2 rows. Break off B yarn. Join 3 strands of A yarn (2 strands of A Pontresina and 1 strand of A Monique) and knit this row, decreasing 1 st each end of needle. Continue working in stockinette st, with knit side as right side, decreasing 1 st each end of needle every other row until 8 (8-8) sts remain. Bind off.

■ **Sleeves:** With Junior Jumbo Jet knitting needles and 3 strands of A yarn, cast on 10 (12-14) sts. Work even in stockinette st with knit side as right side, increasing 1 st each end of needle every 6 (6-6) rows until 18 (20-22 are on the needle. Work even until piece measures 10 (11-12)". Be sure to end with a purl row. Break off A yarn. Join 3 strands of B yarn (2 strands of Pontresina and 1 strand of Monique) and knit this row. Knit next row also. (This will reverse the stockinette st so purl side of B yarn is right side. Work even in stockinette st until 9 (9-9) purl bumps are on right side.

■ **Armhole:** Bind off 2 (2-2) sts at beg of the next 2 rows. Break off B yarn. Join 3 strands of A yarn and knit this row, decreasing 1 st each end of needle. Continue working in stockinette st with knit side as right side, decreasing 1 st each end of needle every other row until 4 (4-4) sts remain. Bind off.

■ **Finishing:** Place pieces of garment so knit sides are together and purl side faces you. With one split strand of Monique, sew side and sleeve seams "bump to bump." Leave B section open. Set sleeves in on wrong side. Turn sweater right side out and with split strand of Monique weave seams together on the right side. With 1 split strand of B Monique work purl "bumps" together on right side. With #K crochet hook and 3 strands of yarn, sc around bottom neck edge and sleeves of sweater.

■ **Note:** If sweater body or sleeves are to be lengthened or shortened, do so before joining B yarn.

Baseball Sweater for Men

Baseball Sweater for Men

■ **Sizes:** Directions are written for small size (36-38). Changes for medium size (40-42) and large size (44-46) are in parentheses.

■ **Materials: Reynolds Monique** 6 (7-7) balls A, **Monique** 6 (7-7) balls B, **Mohair No. 1** 3 (3-3) balls A.

■ **Knitting Needles Required: Reynolds Jumbo Jets.** Aluminum crochet hook size K.

■ **Gauge:** 4 sts = 3½"; 3 rows = 2".

■ **Back:** With Jumbo Jet knitting needles and 3 strands of yarn (1 strand of each kind and color) cast on 20 (22-24) sts. Work even in stockinette st until piece measures 17½ (18-18½)", or desired length to underarm.

■ **Armhole:** Bind off 1 (1-1) st at beg of the next 2 rows. Dec 1 st each end of needle every other row until 6 (8-8) sts remain. Bind off.

■ **Front:** Work same as back.

■ **Sleeves:** With Jumbo Jet knitting needles and 3 strands of yarn (1 strand of each color) cast on 10 (10-12) sts. Work even in stockinette st for 5 (5-5) rows. Inc 1 st each end of needle on next row. Continue to inc 1 st each end of needle every 5th (5th-5th) row until 18 (20-22) sts are on needle. Work even until piece measures 18 (18½-19)", or desired length to underarm.

■ **Armhole:** Bind off 1 (1-1) st at beg of the next 2 rows. Dec 1 st each end of needle every other row until 4 (4-6) sts remain. Bind off.

■ **Finishing:** Place pieces of garment together so right sides face each other, and wrong side faces you. With 1 split strand of Monique, sew sleeve and side seams on wrong side "bump to bump." Set sleeves in this way also. Turn garment right side out and with 1 split strand of Monique weave seams together on right side. With #K crochet hook and 3 strands of yarn, sc around bottom of sweater and sleeves. Using same 3 strands of yarn and #K hook, work 1 row of slip stitch just below the bound-off row around neck edge.

Baseball Sweater for Boys

■ **Sizes:** Directions are written for small size (8). Changes for medium size (10) and large size (12) are in parentheses.

- **Materials:** Reynolds Monique 4 (5-5) balls A, **Monique** 3 (4-4) balls B, Mohair No. 1 2 (2-2) balls A.

- **Knitting Needles Required: Reynolds Junior Jumbo Jets.** Aluminum crochet hook size K.

- **Gauge:** 4 sts = 3"; 5 rows = 2".

- **Back:** With Junior Jumbo Jet knitting needles and 3 strands of yarn (1 strand of each kind and color) cast on 18 (20-22) sts. Work even in stockinette st until piece measures 12 (12½-13)", or desired length to underarm.

- **Armhole:** Bind off 1 (1-1) st at the beg of the next 2 rows. Continue working in stockinette st, decreasing 1 st each end of needle every other row until 6 (8-8) sts remain. Bind off.

- **Front:** Work same as back.

- **Sleeves:** With Junior Jumbo Jet knitting needles and 3 strands of yarn (1 strand of each color) cast on 10 (12-14) sts. Work even in stockinette st for 4 (4-4) rows. **Next row:** Inc 1 st each end of needle. Continue in stockinette st, increasing 1 st each end of needle every 6th (6th-6th) row until 16 (18-20) sts are on needle. Work even until piece measures 12½ (14-15)", or desired length to underarm.

- **Armhole:** Bind off 1 (1-1) st at beg of the next 2 rows. Dec 1 st each end of needle every other row until 4 (6-6) sts remain. Bind off.

- **Finishing:** Place pieces of garment so right sides are together and wrong sides face you. With 1 split strand of Monique, sew side and sleeve seams "bump to bump." Set sleeves in same way. Turn garment right side out. With 1 split strand of yarn, weave seams tog. With #K crochet hook and 3 strands of yarn, sc around hem and sleeves. With same hook and yarn, work 1 row sl st around neck edge just below the bound off sts.

Hockey Sweater for Men

- **Sizes:** Directions are for small size (36-38). Changes for medium size (40-42) and large size (44-46) are in parentheses.

- **Materials:** Reynolds Pontresina 4 (4-5) balls (A), **Pontresina 2** (2-3) balls (B), **Pontresina 1** (1-1) ball (C), **Monique 1** (1-1) ball (C), **Monique 2** (2-3) balls (B), **Monique 3** (3-4) balls (A).
This sweater may be made in any 3 colors of these 2 yarns you choose to combine.

- **Knitting Needles Required: Reynolds Jumbo Jets.** Aluminum crochet hook size K.

- **Gauge:** 6 sts = 5"; 2 rows = 1".

- **Back:** With Jumbo Jet knitting needles and 3 strands of A yarn (2 strands of A Pontresina and 1 strand of A Monique) cast on 22 (24-26) sts. Work even in ribbing (K 1, P 1) for 10½ (11-12)". Continue in following pattern:
Row 1: Knit. **Row 2:** Purl and break A yarn. **Row 3:** Join 3 strands B yarn (2 strands B Pontresina and 1 strand B Monique) purl. **Row 4:** Knit across and break off B. **Row 5:** Join 3 strands of C yarn (2 strands of C Pontresina and 1 strand C Monique), purl. **Row 6:** Purl. **Row 7:** Knit across and break off C yarn. **Row 8:** Join 3 strands of B yarn (2 strands B Pontresina and 1 strand B Monique), knit. **Row 9:** Purl across and break off B yarn. **Row 10:** Join 3 strands of A yarn (2 strands A Pontresina and 1 strand A Monique), knit. **Row 11:** Knit. **Row 12:** Purl across and break off A yarn. **Row 13:** Join 3 strands of B yarn and purl.
Armhole: Continue in stockinette st. Bind off 1 (1-1) st at beginning of the next 2 rows. Dec 1 st each end every other row until 8 (10-10) sts remain. Bind off.

- **Front:** Work same as back.

- **Sleeve:** With Jumbo Jet knitting needles and 3 strands of A yarn, cast on 10 (12-14) sts. Work even in ribbing (K 1, P 1) for 6 (6½-7)". **Next Row:** Increase 1 st each end of needle. Continue to inc 1 st each end of needle every 6th (6th-6th) row until 18 sts (20 sts-22 sts) are on needle, working all new sts in pattern. Continue ribbing until piece measures 13 (13½-14)". Work 13 pattern rows same as back.
Armhole: Continue in stockinette st. Bind off 1 (1-1) st at beginning of next 2 rows. Dec 1 st each end of needle every other row until 4 (6-6) sts remain. Bind off.

- **Finishing:** Place pieces of garment so knit sides are together and purl side faces you. With 1 split strand of Monique sew side and sleeve

Hockey Sweater for Men

seams, "bump to bump." Set sleeves in same way. Turn garment right
side out. With 1 split strand of Monique, weave seams on right side
using colors to match pattern. With a #K crochet hook and 3 strands
of yarn, sc around bottom, sleeves and neck edge of garment.

Hockey Sweater for Boys

■ **Sizes:** Directions are for small size (8). Changes for medium size (10) and large size (12) are in parentheses.

■ **Materials:** Reynolds **Pontresina 3** (3-4) balls (A), **Pontresina 2** (2-3) balls (B), **Pontresina 1** (1-1) ball (C), **Monique 2** (2-3) balls (A), **Monique 2** (2-2) balls (B), **Monique 1** (1-1) ball (C).
This sweater may be made in any 3 color combination you choose to combine in these 2 yarns.

■ **Knitting Needles Required:** Reynolds Junior Jumbo Jets. Aluminum crochet hook size K.

■ **Gauge:** 3 sts = 2"; 7 rows = 3".

■ **Back:** With Junior Jumbo Jet knitting eedles and 3 strands of A yarn (2 strands A Pontresina and 1 strand A Monique) cast on 20 (22-24) sts. Work even in ribbing (K 1, P 1) until piece measures 8 (9-10)". Continue in following pattern: **Row 1:** Knit. **Row 2:** Purl across and break off A yarn. **Row 3:** Join 3 strands of B yarn (2 strands of B Pontresina and 1 strand B Monique), purl. **Row 4:** Knit across and break off B yarn. **Row 5:** Join 3 strands of C yarn (2 strands of C Pontresina and 1 strand C Monique), purl. **Row 6:** Purl. **Row 7:** Knit across and break C yarn. **Row 8:** Join 3 strands of B yarn, knit across. **Row 9:** Purl across and break B yarn. **Row 10:** Join 3 strands of A yarn, knit. **Row 11:** Knit. **Row 12:** Purl across and break A yarn. **Row 13:** Join 3 strands of B yarn and purl across.
Armhole: Continue in stockinette st. Bind off 1 (1-1) st at beginning of next 2 rows. Decrease 1 st each end of needle every other row until 8 (8-10) sts remain. Bind off.

■ **Front:** Work same as back.

■ **Sleeve:** With Junior Jumbo Jet knitting needles and 3 strands of A yarn, cast on 12 (14-16) sts. Work even in ribbing (K 1, P 1) for 3½ (4-4½)". **Next row:** Increase 1 st each end of needle. Continue to increase 1 st each end of needle every 6th (6th-6th) row until 18 (20-22) sts, working all new sts in pattern. Continue in ribbing until piece measures 9 (10-11)". Work 13 pattern rows same as Back.
Armhole: Continue in stockinette st. Bind off 1 (1-1) st at beginning of next 2 rows. Dec 1 st each end of needle every other row until 6 (6-8) sts remain. Bind off.

■ **Finishing:** Place pieces of garment so knit sides are together and purl side faces you. With 1 split strand of Monique, sew side and sleeve seams "bump to bump." Set sleeves in same way. Turn garment right side out. With 1 split strand of Monique, weave seams on right side, using colors to match pattern. With #K crochet hook and 3 strands of yarn, sc around bottom of sweater, sleeves and neck edge.

Checkmate Sweater for Men

■ **Sizes:** Directions are for small size (36-38). Changes for medium size (40-42) and large size (44-46) are in parentheses.

■ **Materials: Reynolds Pontresina** 7 (8-8) balls main color (MC); **Pontresina** 1 (1-1) ball contrasting color (CC); **Monique** 6 (7-7) balls MC; **Monique** 1 (1-1) ball CC.

■ **Knitting Needles Required: Reynolds Jumbo Jets.** Aluminum crochet hook size K.

■ **Gauge:** 2 sts = 1½"; 3 rows = 2".

■ **Back:** Using Reynolds Jumbo Jet knitting needles and 3 strands of MC yarn (2 MC Pontresina and 1 MC Monique), cast on 22 (24-26) sts. Work even in pattern for 4 rows as follows:
Back Pattern St for Small and Large Sizes (22 sts-26 sts)
Row 1: K 2 MC, * K 2 CC, K 2 MC, repeat from * across row.
Row 2: P 2 MC, * P 2 CC, P 2 MC, repeat from * across row.
Row 3: K 2 CC, * K 2 MC, K 2 CC, repeat from * across row.
Row 4: P 2 CC, * P 2 MC, P 2 CC, repeat from * across row.
Back Pattern St for Medium Size (24 sts)
Row 1: K 2 MC, K 2 CC, repeat across row. **Row 2:** P 2 MC, P 2 CC, repeat across row. **Row 3:** K 2 CC, K 2 MC, repeat across row. **Row 4:** P 2 CC, P 2 MC, repeat across row.
Break off CC yarn. Continuing with MC, work even in stockinette st until piece measures 16 (16½-17½)" or desired length to underarm.
Armhole: Bind off 2 (2-2) sts at beginning of the next 2 rows. Continue working in stockinette st, decreasing 1 st each end of needle every other row until 8 (10-10) sts remain. Bind off.

■ **Front:** With Reynolds Jumbo Jet knitting needles and 3 strands of MC yarn (2 MC Pontresina and 1 MC Monique) cast on 22 (24-26) sts. Work even in pattern for 4 (4-4) rows as follows:
Front Pattern St for Large and Small Sizes (22 sts-26 sts)
Row 1: K 2 CC, * K 2 MC, K 2 CC, repeat from * across row.
Row 2: P 2 CC, * P 2 MC, P 2 CC, repeat from * across row.
Row 3: K 2 MC, * K 2 CC, K 2 MC, repeat from * across row.
Row 4: P 2 MC, * P 2 CC, P 2 MC, repeat from * across row.
Front Pattern St for Medium Size—same as Back Medium Size pattern.
Break off CC yarn. Continuing with MC, work even in stockinette st until piece measures 16 (16½-17½)", or desired length to underarm.
Armhole: Bind off 2 (2-2) sts at beginning of the next 2 rows. Decrease 1 st each end every other row until 8 (10-10) sts remain. Bind off.

■ **Sleeves:** With Reynolds Jumbo Jet knitting needles and 3 strands of

Checkmate Sweater for Men

MC yarn, cast on 10 (10-12) sts. Work even in pattern for 4 rows as follows:

Sleeve Pattern St for Small and Medium Sizes—follow pattern for Small and Large Back sizes.

Sleeve Pattern St for Large Size—follow pattern for Medium Back and Front sizes.

Break off CC yarn. Continue using MC yarn. Inc evenly across row until you have 13 (15-17) sts on needle. Work even until piece measures 11 (12-13)". Inc 1 st each end of needle. Work even for 4 (4-4) rows more. Inc 1 st each end of needle. Work even on 17 (19-21) sts until piece measures 18 (18½-19)". End with a purl row.

Armhole: Bind off 2 (2-2) sts at the beg of the next 2 rows. Decrease 1 st each end of needle every other row until 5 (5-5) sts remain. Bind off.

Checkmate Sweater for Boys

■ **Sizes:** Directions are for small size (8). Changes for medium size (10) and large size (12) are in parentheses.
Fits Chest Size: 26 (28-30)".

■ **Materials: Reynolds Pontresina** 5 (6-6) balls main color (MC); **Pontresina** 1 (1-1) ball contrasting color (CC); **Monique** 4 (5-5) balls MC; **Monique** 1 (1-1) ball CC.

■ **Knitting Needles Required: Reynolds Junior Jumbo Jets.** Aluminum crochet hook size K.

■ **Gauge:** 4 sts = 3"; 2 rows = 1".

■ **Back:** With Reynolds Junior Jumbo Jet knitting needles and 3 strands of MC yarn (2 strands MC Pontresina and 1 strand MC Monique) cast on 18 (20-22) sts. K 2 MC sts. Join 3 strands of CC (2 strands CC Pontresina and 1 strand CC Monique) and follow pattern given for correct size.

Back Pattern St for Small and Large Sizes (8-12)
Row 1: K 2 MC, * K 2 CC, K 2 MC, repeat from * across row.
Row 2: P 2 MC, * P 2 CC, P 2 MC, repeat from * across row.
Row 3: K 2 CC, * K 2 MC, K 2 CC, repeat from * across row.
Row 4: P 2 CC, * P 2 MC, P 2 CC, repeat from * across row.

Back Pattern St for Medium Size (10)
Row 1: K 2 MC, K 2 CC, repeat across row. **Row 2:** P 2 MC, P 2 CC, repeat across row. **Row 3:** K 2 CC, K 2 MC, repeat across row. **Row 4:** P 2 CC, P 2 MC, repeat across row.

Break off CC yarn. Using MC only, work even in stockinette st until piece measures 12 (13-14)" or desired length to underarm.

Armhole: Bind off 2 (2-2) sts at beginning of the next 2 rows. Decrease 1 st each end of needle every other row until 6 (6-8) sts remain. Bind off.

■ **Front:** Work same as Back, using same pattern st for Medium Size (10) as given for Back, but using new pattern st for Small Size (8) and Large Size (12).

Front Pattern St for Sizes 8 and 12

Row 1: K 2 CC, * K 2 MC, K 2 CC, repeat from * across row.
Row 2: P 2 CC, * P 2 MC, P 2 CC, repeat from * across row.
Row 3: K 2 MC, * K 2 CC, K 2 MC, repeat from * across row.
Row 4: P 2 MC, * P 2 CC, P 2 MC, repeat from * across row.

Break off CC yarn. Using MC only, work even in stockinette st until piece measures 12 (13-14)". Finish same as back.

■ **Sleeves:** With Reynolds Junior Jumbo Jet knitting needles and 3 strands of MC yarn (2 MC Pontresina and 1 MC Monique) cast on 12 (12-12) sts. K 2 sts MC. Join 3 strands CC yarn and follow pattern as given for Medium Size Back, until 4 rows are completed. Break off CC yarn. Using MC only, inc evenly across next row to 15 (17-19) sts. Work in stockinette st until piece measures 10 (11-12½)". Inc 1 st each end of next row. Work even until piece measures 12½ (13½-15)".

Armhole: Bind off 2 (2-2) sts at beginning of next 2 rows. Decrease 1 st each end of needle every other row until 5 (5-7) sts remain. Bind off.

■ **Finishing:** Place pieces of garment so knit sides are together and purl side faces you. With 1 split strand of Monique, sew side and sleeve seams "bump to bump" on wrong side. Set sleeves in same way. Turn garment right side out and with 1 split strand of Monique weave side, sleeve, and raglan seams. With #K crochet hook and 3 strands of yarn, sc around bottom edge and sleeves. Work 1 row sl st around neck edge just below bound-off sts.

Spectator Sweater for Men

■ **Sizes:** Directions are for small size (36-38). Changes for medium size (40-42) and large size (44-46) are in parentheses.

■ **Materials: Reynolds Monique** 13 (14-14) balls, **Versailles** 3 (3-3) balls. This sweater may be made in any colors of these 2 yarns you choose to combine.

■ **Knitting Needles Required: Reynolds Jumbo Jets.** Aluminum crochet hook size K.

■ **Gauge:** 12 sts = 11"; 5 rows = 3".

■ **Pattern: Pattern Stitch for Back and Front—**
Row 1: K 3 (4-5) P 2, K 4, P 2, K 4, P 2, K 3 (4-5). **Row 2:** P 3 (4-5), K 2, P 4, K 2, P 4, K 2, P 3 (4-5). Repeat these 2 rows for pattern.

■ **Back:** With Jumbo Jet knitting needles and 3 strands of yarn (2 strands of Monique and 1 strand of Versailles) cast 20 (22-24) sts. Work even in pattern until piece measures 16½ (17½-18)", or desired length to underarm.
Armhole: Bind off 1 (1-1) st at beg of the next 2 rows. Keeping pattern as established, dec 1 st each end of needle every other row until 8 (8-10) sts remain. Bind off.

■ **Front:** Same as back.

■ **Sleeves: Pattern Stitch for Sleeves—**
Row 1: K 4 (4-5), P 2, K 4 (4-5). **Row 2:** P 4 (4-5), K 2, P 4 (4-5). Repeat these 2 rows for sleeve pattern.
With Jumbo Jet knitting needles and 3 strands of yarn (2 strands of Monique and 1 strand of Versailles) cast on 10 (10-12) sts. Work even in sleeve pattern, increasing 1 st each end of needle every 6th (6th-6th) row until 18 (20-22) sts on needle. (Work all added sts in stockinette st.) Work even in pattern until 17 (18-19)", or desired length to underarm.
Armholes: Bind off 1 (1-1) st at the beg of the next 2 rows. Continue in pattern, decreasing 1 st each end of needle every other row until 6 (6-8) sts remain. Bind off.

■ **Finishing:** Place pieces of garment so knit sides are together and purl side faces you. With 1 split strand of Monique, sew side and sleeve "bump to bump." Set sleeves in same way. Turn garment right side out and weave seams together. Shape raglan seam. With a #K crochet hook and 3 strands of yarn, sc around bottom of sweater and sleeves. With same hook and yarn, work 1 row sl st around neck edge, just below the bound off sts.

Spectator Sweater for Men

Spectator Sweater for Boys

- **Sizes:** Directions are for small size (8). Changes for medium size (10) and large size (12) are in parentheses.

- **Materials: Reynolds Monique** 9 (10-10) balls, Versailles 2 (2-2) balls. This sweater may be made in any colors of these 2 yarns you choose to combine.

- **Knitting Needles Required: Reynolds Junior Jumbo Jets.** Aluminum crochet hook size K.

- **Gauge:** 4 sts = 3"; 5 rows = 2".

- **Pattern Stitch: Row 1:** K 2 (3-4), P 2, K 4, P 2, K 4, P 2, K 2 (3-4). **Row 2:** P 2 (3-4), K 2, P 4, K 2, P 4, K 2, P 2 (3-4). Repeat these 2 rows for pattern.

- **Back:** With Junior Jumbo Jet knitting needles and 3 strands of yarn (2 strands of Monique and 1 strand of Versailles) cast on 18 (20-22) sts. Work even in pattern until piece measures 11½ (13-14)", or desired length to underarm.
Armhole: Bind off 1 (1-1) st at the beg of the next 2 rows. Continue in pattern as already established, decreasing 1 st each end of needle every other row until 8 (8-10) sts remain. Bind off.

- **Front:** Work same as back.

- **Sleeve: Pattern Stitch for Sleeve—Row 1:** K 4 (5-6), P 2, K 4 (5-6). **Row 2:** P 4 (5-6), K 2, P 4 (5-6). Repeat these 2 rows.
With Junior Jumbo Jet knitting needles and 3 strands of yarn (2 strands of Monique and 1 strand of Versailles) cast on 10 (12-14) sts. Work in sleeve pattern, increasing 1 st each end of needle every 6th (6th-6th) row until 16 (18-20) sts on needle. (Keep all new sts in stockinette st.) Work even until work mesures 13 (14-15)", or desired length to underarm.
Armhole: Bind off 1 (1-1) st at beg of the next 2 rows. Continuing in pattern established, dec 1 st each end of needle every other row until 4 (4-6) sts remain. Bind off.

- **Finishing:** Place pieces of garment so knit sides are together and purl side faces you. With 1 split strand of Monique, sew side and sleeve "bump to bump." Set sleeves in same way. Turn garment right side out and weave together. Shape raglan seam. With a #K crochet hook and 3 strands of yarn, sc around bottom of sweater and sleeves. With same hook and yarn, work 1 row sl st around neck edge, just below the bound off sts.

Striped Soccer Sweater for Men

■ **Sizes:** Directions are for small size (36-38). Changes for medium size (40-42) and large size (44-46) are in parentheses.

■ **Materials: Reynolds Pontresina,** 2 (3-3) balls each of #5031 and #5025 for color A; **Pontresina** #5036, 2 (2-2) balls color B; **Monique** #1713, **4** (5-5) balls color A; **Monique** #1705, 2 (3-3) balls color B; **Chanson de Paris** #4008, 2 (2-2) balls color B. **Note:** If Chanson is not available substitute Versailles #583, 2 (2-2) balls color B.

■ **Knitting Needles Required: Reynolds Jumbo Jets.** Aluminum crochet hook size K.

■ **Gauge:** 6 sts = 5"; 7 rows = 4".

■ **Back:** With Reynolds Jumbo Jets and 1 strand of each A color yarn (2 A Pontresina and 1 A Monique) cast on 22 (24-26) sts. Work even in stockinette st for 8 (10-10) rows. Carry color yarn not in use up side, locking every second row. Drop A yarn. Join 1 strand of each B color yarn (1 Chanson, 1 Monique, and I Pontresina). With B yarn, work **8** (8-8) rows. Drop B, pick up A, work 8 (8-8) rows. Drop A, pick up B.
Armhole: Bind off 1 (1-1) st at beg of next 2 rows. Work even in B for 6 (6-6) rows more. Break off B yarn. Pick up A yarn and work 6 (8-8) rows.
Neck Opening: Using A yarn, K 7 (8-8) sts. Bind off 6 (6-8) sts. K 7 (8-8) sts. Work both sides at same time, using 2 lots of yarn. Turn and P 7 (8-8) sts. Attach 3 strands of A yarn at neck edge and P last 7 (8-8) sts. Turn. K 7 (8-8) sts. Drop yarn. Pick up second yarns and K 7 (8-8) sts. Turn.

■ **Front:** P 7 (8-8) sts. Cast on 6 (6-8) sts for neck. Purl across last 7 (8-8) sts. You will have 20 (22-24) sts now on needle. Continuing with A yarn, work 6 (8-8) rows. Join B yarn and work for 6 (6-6) rows. **(Front Armhole:)** **Row 7:** Cast on 1 (1-1) st at beg of row. Knit across. **Row 8:** Cast on 1 (1-1) st at beg of row and purl across. (Continuing **Front:**) Drop B yarn, pick up A yarn, and work 8 (8-8) rows. Drop A yarn; pick up B yarn, and work 8 (8-8) rows. Break off B yarn. Pick up A yarn and work 8 (10-10) rows. Bind off.

■ **Sleeves:** With Reynolds Jumbo Jets and 1 strand of each A color yarn (2 A Pontresina and 1 A Monique) cast on 10 (10-12) sts. Work even in stockinette st for 4 rows. Inc 1 st each end of needle on 5th row, all sizes, and every 6th (4th-4th) row until 18 (20-22) sts on needle; **at same time,** when there are 12 (14-16) rows of A, join 3 strands of B yarn and work 8 (8-8) rows. Drop B yarn, pick up A yarn, and work 8 (8-8) rows. Drop A yarn, pick up B yarn.

Armhole: Bind off 1 (1-2) sts at beg of the next 2 rows Dec 1 st each

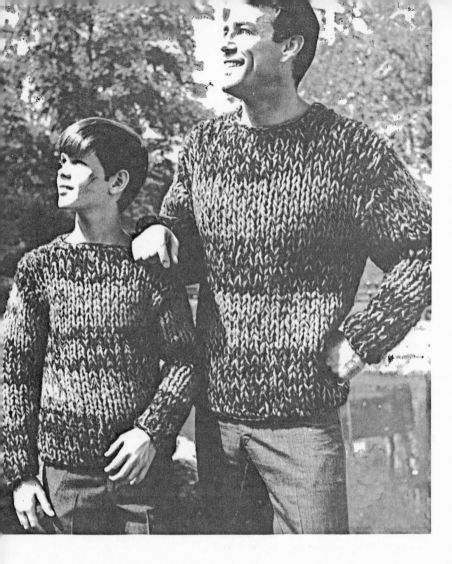

Striped Soccer Sweater for Men

end of needle every other row until 8 (10-10) sts remain. At same time, when there are 8 (8-8) rows of B, break off B yarn and pick up A yarn. Work 2 rows of A and bind off last 8 (10-10) sts.

■ **Finishing:** Place pieces of garment so knit sides are together and purl side faces you. With 1 split strand of Monique, sew side and sleeve seams (using color yarn to match pattern) "bump to bump." Set sleeves in same way. Turn garment right side out. With 1 split strand of Monique in correct color, weave seams on right side. With #K crochet hook, sc around bottom of sweater, sleeves, and neck edge.

Striped Soccer Sweater for Boys

■ **Sizes:** Directions are for small size (8). Changes for medium size (10) and large size (12) are in parentheses.
Fits Chest Size: 26 (28-30)".

■ **Materials: Reynolds Pontresina,** 1 (2-2) balls each of #5031 and #5025 for color A; **Pontresina** #5036, 1 (1-1) ball color B; **Monique** #1713, 2 (3-3) balls color A; **Monique** #1705, 1 (2-2) balls color B; **Chanson de Paris** #4008, 1 (1-1) ball color B. **Note:** If Chanson is not available substitute Versailles #583, 2 (2-2) balls color B.

■ **Knitting Needles Required: Reynolds Junior Jumbo Jets.** Aluminum crochet hook size K.

■ **Gauge:** 3 sts = 2"; 7 rows = 3".

■ **Back:** With Reynolds Junior Jumbo Jets and 1 strand of each A color yarn (2 strands of A Pontresina and 1 strand A Monique) cast on 18 (20-22) sts. Work even in stockinette st 8 (10-12) rows. Drop A yarn. Join 1 strand each of B color yarn (1 strand Chanson, 1 strand Pontresina and 1 strand Monique). Carry yarn not being used up side of work, locking every other row. With B yarn work 8 (8-8) rows. Drop B yarn. Pick up A yarn and work 8 (8-8) rows. Drop A yarn and pick up B yarn.
Armholes: Bind off 1 st at beg of next 2 rows. Continue in B yarn for 6 (6-6) more rows. Break off B. Pick up A yarn and work 4 (6-6) rows.
Neck Opening: Continuing with A yarn, K 5 (5-6) sts. Bind off 6 (8-8) sts. K last 5 (5-6) sts. Work both sides at same time, using 2 lots of yarn: Turn and P 5 (5-6) sts. Attach 3 strands of A yarn at neck edge and P remaining 5 (5-6) sts. Turn. K 5 (5-6) sts, drop yarn, pick up second yarns and K 5 (5-6) sts. Turn.

■ **Front:** P 5 (5-6) sts. Cast on 6 (8-8) sts for neck. P across last 5 (5-6) sts with same yarn. Break off the spare yarn. 16 (18-20) sts on needle. Continuing with A yarn, work even 4 (6-6) rows. Join 3 strands of B yarn. Work even 6 (6-6) rows. **(Front Armhole:) Row 7:** Cast on 1 (1-1) st at beg of row. Knit across. **Row 8:** Cast on 1 (1-1) st at beg of row and purl across. You will have 18 (20-22) sts on needle. (Continuing **Front:)** Drop B yarn. Pick up A yarn and work 8 (8-8) rows. Drop A yarn and pick up B yarn, and work 8 (8-8) rows. Break off B yarn and pick up A yarn, and work 8 (10-12) rows. Bind off.

■ **Sleeves:** With Reynolds Junior Jumbo Jets and 1 strand of each A color yarn, cast on 10 (12-14) sts. Work in stockinette st for 4 rows. Inc 1 st each end of needle on 5th row, all sizes, and every 4th (5th-5th) row until 20 (22-24) sts; **at same time,** when there are 10 (12-14) rows of A, join 3 strands of B yarn and work 8 rows. Drop B yarn, pick up A, and work 8 rows. Drop A yarn, pick up B yarn.
Armholes: At beg of next 2 rows, bind off 1 (1-2) sts. Decrease 1 st each end of needle every other row until 8 (10-10) sts remain; **at same time,** when there are 8 (8-8) rows of B, break off B yarn, pick up A yarn, and work 2 rows. Bind off last 8 (10-10) sts.

■ **Finishing:** Place pieces of garment so knit sides are together and purl side faces you. With 1 split strand of Monique, sew side and sleeve seams (using color yarn to match pattern) "bump to bump." Set sleeves in same way. Turn garment right side out. With 1 split strand of Monique

Star Tweed Sweater

Star Tweed Sweater

- **Sizes:** Directions are for small size (36-38). Changes for medium size (40-42) and large size (44-46) are in parentheses.

- **Materials: Reynolds Plumage,** 4 (5-5) balls; **Reynolds Monique** in co-ordinating colors, 6 (7-7) balls each of A and B.

- **Knitting Needles Required: Reynolds Jumbo Jets.** Aluminum crochet hook size K.

- **Gauge:** 8 sts = 7"; 7 rows = 4".

- **Pattern Stitch:** To be worked on center 7 sts of Front and Sleeves. **Row 1:** P 7 sts. **Row 2:** K 3, P 1, K 3. **Row 3:** P 2, K 3, P 2. **Row 4:** K 1, P 5, K 1. **Row 5:** P 2, K 3, P 2. **Row 6:** K 3, P 1, K 3. Repeat these 6 rows for pattern.

- **Back:** Using Jumbo Jet knitting needles and 3 strands of yarn (1 of each color) cast on 21 (23-25) sts. Work in stockinette st until 16 (17-18)" in all, or desired length to underarm.
Armholes: Bind off 1 (1-1) st at beg of the next 2 rows. Dec 1 st each end every other row until 7 (7-9) sts remain. Bind off.

- **Front:** Using Jumbo Jet knitting needles and 3 strands of yarn (1 of each color) cast on 21 (23-25) sts. **Row 1:** K 7 (8-9) sts. Work row 1 of pattern over next 7 sts; K 7 (8-9) sts. Keeping the center 7 sts of all sizes in pattern st and the 7 (8-9) sts on each side in stockinette st, work until 16 (17-18)" in all or desired length to underarm.
Armholes: Bind off 1 (1-1) st at beg of the next 2 rows. Dec 1 st each end every other row until 7 (7-9) sts remain. Bind off.

- **Sleeves:** Using Jumbo Jet knitting needles and 3 strands of yarn (1 of each color) cast on 11 (13-13) sts. **Row 1:** K 2 (3-3) sts. Work row 1 of pattern over center 7 sts. K 2 (3-3) sts. **Row 2:** P 2 (3-3) sts. Work row 2 of pattern over center 7 sts. P 2 (3-3) sts. Continuing to keep center 7 sts in pattern and all other sts in stockinette st, inc 1 st each end of needle every 6 (6-5)" until 15 (17-19) sts. Work even until sleeve measures 17½ (18-19)" or desired length to underarm.
Armholes: Bind off 1 (1-1) st at beg of next 2 rows. Dec 1 st each end every other row until 3 (3-5) sts remain. Bind off.

- **Finishing:** With right sides together and wrong side facing you, with 1 split strand of Monique weave side, sleeve and raglan seams together. Turn work right side out and reweave seams on right side, keeping seams flat. Using 3 strands of yarn and #K crochet hook, work 1 row sc around bottom and sleeve edges. Work 1 row sl st around neck edge just below bound off sts.

Dresses for Girls

Ribbon Candy

Sizes: Directions are written for small size 8. Changes for medium size (10) and large size (12) are in parentheses.
Materials: 1 pair **Reynolds Junior Jumbo Jet** knitting needles; 1 #J aluminum crochet hook; 1 ping-pong ball; **Scotch Mist** #504 (2); **Scotch Mist** #7269 (2); **Scotch Mist** #72160 (2); **Royale Crylor** #581 (2); **Classique** #2500 (2); **Classique** #2534 (2); **Classique** #2511 (2); **Pontresina** #5021 (2); **Pontresina** #5036 (2); **Pontresina** #5033 (2); **Monte Carlo** #4600 (2); **Monte Carlo** #4625 (2).

■ **Gauge:** 5 sts = 3"; 2 rows = 1".
Pattern: Stockinette st in striping pattern: 4 rows green, 2 rows red, 4 rows white, 2 rows red. Note: Do not break off yarns not in use. Carry them up along edge, locking every 2nd row.

■ **Back:** Using Reynolds Junior Jumbo Jet knitting needles and 4 strands of yarn (1 of each kind in each color) cast on 24 (26-28) sts. Start with 4 rows of green and, keeping striping pattern as given, work until piece measures 16½ (17½-18½) inches, or desired length to underarm.
Armhole: Bind off 2 (2-2) sts at beg of the next 2 rows. Work 2 (2-2) rows even. (Be sure to keep sriping pattern.) Dec 1 st each end every other row until 6 (6-8) sts remain. Bind off loosely.

■ **Front:** Work same as Back. Be sure to start armhole on same striping pattern row as the Back.

■ **Sleeves:** Using Reynolds Junior Jumbo Jet knitting needles and 4 strands of green yarn (1 of each kind) cast on 8 (10-12) sts. Work in striping pattern, increasing 1 st each end on first red stripe and again on second green stripe (all sizes). 12 (14-16) sts are on needle. Continue in striping pattern until sleeve measures 12½ (13½-15) inches, or desired length to underarm. Be sure to start armhole shaping on same striping row as body of sweater.
Armhole: Bind off 1 (1-1) st at beg of the next 2 rows. Work 2 rows even. Dec 1 st each end of next row. Work 4 rows even. Dec 1 st each end of next row. From now on dec 1 st each end every other row until 4 (4-4) sts remain. Bind off loosely.

■ **Collar:** With Junior Jumbo Jet knitting needles and 4 strands of red yarn cast on 22 (24-24) sts. Work in stockinette st for 5 rows. Bind off.

■ **Finishing:** With right sides of dress together, wrong side facing you, using 1 strand of Royale Crylor or Monte Carlo in the color to be joined, weave side, sleeve and raglan seams. Turn dress right side out and using same color yarn reweave seams, keeping work flat. Fold collar in half

Ribbon Candy

lengthwise, having purl side as right side. Weave seams, using 1 strand of Monte Carlo in red. Using #J crochet hook and 4 strands of red yarn, make a chain on one end for button loop. Cover ping pong ball with 2 strands each of red, white and green, using the fine yarns (Scotch Mist, Royale Crylor, and Monte Carlo). See note on Ping-Pons in General Information. Sew Ping-pon to the other end of collar for button. Sew collar to neck edge with button in front. Using #J crochet hook and 4 strands of green yarn, work 1 row sc around bottom of dress and sleeves.

Little Girl's Puff Sleeve Dress

Little Girl's Puff Sleeve Dress

■ **Sizes:** Directions are for size 6X. Sizes (8) and (10) are in parentheses.

■ **Materials:** Reynolds **Pontresina,** 4 (5-5) balls; Reynolds **Danskyarn** in matching color, 2 (2-2) balls. This dress can be made in any colors of these 2 yarns.

■ **Knitting Needles Required: Reynolds Junior Jumbo Jets.** Aluminum crochet hook size K.

■ **Gauge:** 3 sts = 2"; 7 rows = 3".

■ **Back:** Using Reynolds Junior Jumbo Jet knitting needles and 3 strands of yarn (2 strands Pontresina and 1 strand Danskyarn) cast on 24 (26-28) sts. K first row into back of each st. Continue in stockinette st for 6 more rows. Purl side is right side, and there will be 7 purl "bumps." Knit the next row to reverse stockinette st pattern. Right side will be the knit side from now on. Continue in stockinette st until 15 (16-17)" in all, or desired length to underarm.
Armholes: Bind off 1 (1-1) st at beginning of next 2 rows. Decrease 1 st each end of needle every other row until 14 (14-16) sts remain. Purl back. Bind off next row, making another decrease by knitting the first 2 sts and last 2 sts together as you bind off.

■ **Front:** Work same as back until there are 16 (16-18) sts remaining. Purl back and bind off same as back.

■ **Sleeves:** Purl side is right side. Using Reynolds Junior Jumbo Jet knitting needles and 3 strands of yarn, cast on 14 (16-18) sts. Purl the first row. **Next row:** K 1 (2-3) sts, K into front and back of each of the next 12 sts, K 1 (2-3) sts (12 increases). There are 26 (28-30) sts on needle. * Purl 1 row. Knit 1 row. On size 10 only, repeat from * once more.
Armholes: Bind off 1 (1-1) st at the beginning of the next 2 rows. **Next row:** P 0 (0-1) st. * P 2 tog, P 1. Repeat from *, ending P 1 (P 2 tog-P 1). Knit the next row. P 2 tog across next row. **Next row:** knit across, decreasing 1 st each end of needle. Size 6X, bind off next row. Sizes 8 and 10, purl 1 row. Knit across next row, decreasing 1 st each end of needle. Bind off.

■ **Finishing:** Using 1 strand of Danskyarn, weave side and sleeve seams (**purl** side of sleeve is right side). See General Information. With #K crochet hook and 3 strands of yarn, work 1 row sc around neck edge, sleeves, and bottom of dress.

Little Girl's Panel Dress

■ **Sizes:** Directions are written for small size (6). Changes for medium size (8) and large size (10) are in parentheses.

■ **Materials: Reynolds Monique,** 3 (4-4) balls main color (MC); 2 (2-2) balls contrasting color (CC); **Reynolds Mohair No. 1,** 2 (3-3) balls MC and 1 (1-1) ball CC.

■ **Knitting Needles Required:** 1 pair Reynolds **Junior Jumbo Jet** knitting needles; 1 #K aluminum crochet hook.
IMPORTANT: Before starting dress, see Helpful Hints and Sizing.

■ **Gauge:** 5 sts = 3"; 2 rows = 1".

■ **Back:** Using Reynolds Junior Jumbo Jet knitting needles and 1 strand of each CC yarn (2 strands) cast on 26 (28-30) sts. Starting with a knit row, work in stockinette st until there are 5 purl "bumps" (5 rows). Purl side is right side. Break off CC. Tie in 2 strands of MC. Knit next row to reverse stockinette st. Continue in stockinette st until work measures 4 (5-5)". **Next row,** dec 1 st each end of needle. Work even in stockinette st for 4 (4-5)". Repeat dec row. Work even for 4 (4-5)". Repeat dec row. 20 (22-24) sts. Work even until piece measures 15 (17-18½)" in all or desired length to underarm.
Armhole: Bind off 1 (1-1) st at beg of the next 2 rows. Work 2 rows even. Dec 1 st each end every other row until 8 (8-10) sts remain. Bind off.

■ **Front:** Cast on and work bottom band same as Back (5 purl "bumps"). Break off CC. Tie in 2 strands of MC (1 of each kind). Knit next row to reverse stockinette st pattern—K 11 (12-13) sts. Tie in CC yarn and P next 4 sts all sizes. Tie in 2nd MC yarn (2 strands) and K last 11 (12-13) sts. Keep pattern as established—11 (12-13) sts in stockinette st, 4 sts in reverse stockinette st, and 11 (12-13) sts in stockinette st. When work measures 4 (5-5)", dec 1 st each end of needle. Work even in pattern for 4 (4-5)". Repeat dec row. Work even in pattern for 4 (4-5)". Repeat dec row. 20 (22-24) sts. Work even until piece measures 15 (17-18½)" in all, or desired length to underarm.
Armhole: Bind off 1 (1-1) st at beg of the next 2 rows. Work 2 rows even. Dec 1 st each end of needle every other row until 8 (8-10) sts remain. Bind off.

■ **Sleeves:** Using Reynolds Junior Jumbo Jet knitting needles and 2 strands of CC (1 of each) cast on 12 (14-16) sts. Work in stockinette st for 5 rows (5 purl "bumps" on right side). Break off CC. Tie on 2 strands of MC and knit next row reverse stockinette st. Continue in stockinette st. Purl 1 row.
Armhole: Bind off 1 (1-1) st at beg of the next 2 rows. Work 2 rows even. Dec 1 st each end of needle until there are 4 sts remaining. Bind off.

Little Girl's Panel Dress

■ **Collar:** Using Reynolds Junior Jumbo Jet knitting needles and 2 strands of CC yarn, cast on 23 (25-25) sts. Work in stockinette st for 4 rows (4 purl "bumps" on right side). Bind off.

■ **Finishing:** With right sides of work together and wrong side facing you, join side, sleeve and raglan seams using colors to match work. Turn work right side out and weave seams tog again. Using #K crochet hook, work I row sc around collar. Work 1 row sl st just below sc row on one long edge, holding collar in to fit neck edge of dress. Sew collar to neck edge, with each end of collar at side of center panel. See picture.